TEXTING WOMEN

Phone Number To Date Every Time

Second Edition

By

David Thorpe

Copyright © 2024 David Thorpe Dating

All rights reserved. No part of this book may be reproduced or used in any manner without the prior written permission of the copyright owner.

To protect the anonymity of individuals, elements of the book have been censored.

Second edition

David Thorpe Dating

ISBN: 978-0-646-87664-1

https://www.davidthorpedating.com

Dedication

To all men who refuse to conform, who seek to be more masculine, and who strive for betterment in their pursuit of women. This book is dedicated to you.

Acknowledgements

I WOULD LIKE TO PAY TRIBUTE to a certain Kiwi who gave suggestions for this book's content on nightly coronavirus walks, helped with image annotations and delivered a solid front cover. I would also like to thank the Shakespearean Ed for his masterful eye and editing skills. Thank you both.

Contents

Acknowledgements..v

Introduction..xi

What messaging applications should I use?..........xv

Use my texts..xix

1. The Texting Ladder.................................. 1
2. Easy things you can do to win at Texting.......... 15
   - 2. 1. *Say my name say my name!*................. 15
   - 2. 2. *Write like Shakespeare, not like Trump*........ 18
   - 2. 3. *Paralysis analysis – the use of notes*......... 20
   - 2. 4. *Ellipsis...*.. 21
   - 2. 5. *Ask less questions*............................. 22
   - 2. 6. *What time is it Mr Thorpe?*.................. 23
   - 2. 7. *Go fast or go slow? Mirroring and Crescendos*.................. 25
3. In the beginning, there was the street ping......... 33
4. Shit tests and how to pass them 41
5. Push-Pull.. 51
6. Vacuuming 57
7. Using Photos and Images 65

8. The Holy Grail of Texting – the Audio Message... 75

9. After the first date: When and what to text........ 87

10. How not to text.................................... 93

11. Managing Psycho Girls Over Text................. 99

12. Broadcast Lists 103

13. Phone Calls 107

14. Nao Entendo – Girls Who Don't Speak Your Language 113

15. How to break up over text........................ 117

16. Transitioning from Internet Dating Apps to Texting... 123

17. Thorpe's Texting Clinic – Troubleshooting...... 127

    17. 1. She won't text me back!..................... 127

    17. 2. Her number doesn't work/I can't find her in my messaging app............................... 130

    17. 3. I didn't get her phone number, but I got her Facebook/Instagram/Email/LinkedIn. Do I still follow the chapters in this book? .. 131

    17. 4. She rejected my date request, now what? ... 132

    17. 5. How do I know if she has read my messages? 132

    17. 6. I think I broke the conversation by being too needy or too smart. How do I fix this? ... 133

    17. 7. I've got a date coming up and she hasn't entirely confirmed. Should I text her? 134

    17. 8. Should I text her on the day of the date?..... 135

17. 9. She won't agree to my date location and wants to go somewhere else. What should I do? 136

17. 10. The conversation has hit a dead end. What should I do? 138

17. 11. She's sending me one-word answers and making it difficult. What should I do? 139

17. 12. I literally have no idea what to do next, help! 140

17. 13. She's texting loads and super interested, how do I not mess it up? 141

17. 14. I'm on holiday for a few days and don't feel I have the time to follow the Texting Ladder structure. Is there a way I can fast track the process and get women out on dates so I don't run out of time? 142

17. 15. She's not texting back and I think the lead is dead. Is there anything more I can do to try and revive the conversation? . 143

18. Putting It All Together - In Closing 147

Review This Book 151

YouTube & Social Media 153

More Dating Resources 155

About the Author 159

Contact Me 163

Introduction

THIS BOOK IS FOR MEN who want to improve their texting with women. Whatever your texting experience, there's something in this book for you. From complete beginners to texting Lotharios, I'll teach you everything you need to know to become a well-rounded, accomplished texter in your pursuit of women. If you can improve your texting, you will be seen as an attractive man who gets it and who women want to be with. The foundation of this book is centred on my tried and tested texting structure, the Texting Ladder. A fail-safe, universal structure, the Texting Ladder will be your guide that will radically transform your texting abilities. The Texting Ladder was born from years of texting over a thousand women; trying what worked and what didn't and then evolving these trials and tribulations into a highly efficient system. Accompanying this, I'll teach you the essential tools and techniques that should be in every man's texting arsenal to engage with women as they wish to be engaged with. Finally, I have a chapter on troubleshooting and typical problems men experience during texting.

So why write this book? Once conquering my own dating life years ago, I was possessed by a strong desire to help men in their pursuit of women. I also remember my life from a time before; a time where I was clueless with women and texting, the sting of rejection, and the silence of no reply from that woman I really wanted to meet. Texting is often overlooked as an insignificant part of a man's pursuit of women, but I'm sure most men can relate to doing something wrong over a text and ruining their relationship with a woman they want to be with. However, texting is a skill that can be learned to a good level in a short space of time.

So, let's look at texting. Texting is one of the four cornerstones of a man's pursuit of women.

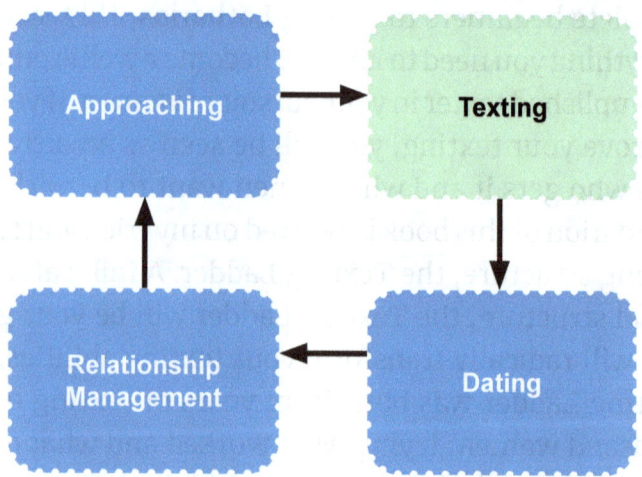

Figure 1. Cornerstones of a man's pursuit of women

Sandwiched between approaching and dating, texting is often neglected by the untrained eye and accompanied with a relaxed attitude of, *"It's just texting, how hard can it be?"* However, such a man will quickly realise the fallacy of holding such a view when he doesn't get a reply to his text and is consequently archived or blocked by his perfect woman. Texting is the bridge between getting a number to going on a date. Once you have an established relationship with a woman through dating, texting is your means to maintaining contact and arranging further dates as part of your relationship management. Try as you might to avoid it, you need to text if you want to go on dates with hot women.

A text message is, in its own right, insignificant. A tiny 140 bytes in size, free to send and instantly transmitted, they are indeed simple. But it's down to you as to how you craft and use them to engage and attract women. Done correctly, you'll be amazed at what texting can do for your relationships with women.

So, texting rightfully takes its place as a cornerstone of your pursuit of women. And you must get good at it if you want results. Get it right and you'll be going on dates with the women of your dreams. Get it wrong and you'll be texting just as many pointless numbers as a LinkedIn Recruiter.

Whilst I'm proud of this comprehensive and detailed book, I appreciate it's easy to feel overwhelmed or lost, especially when you are starting out. But let just one motto stay with you at all times when you are texting.

"Texting is a means to get women out on dates."

That is the objective of texting. It's that simple. Now say it again to yourself.

Nearly all men get hung up on not knowing what to text and make things more complicated than they need to be. But with this book and that motto, you'll start to see what texting is. It's a skill that needs to demonstrate confidence and simplicity whilst also doing the bare minimum to advance the conversation until it's time to go on a date. You need to accept that learning how to text is going to be hard work, takes perseverance, and that you will make mistakes and lose the woman. But's that life and it's the only way you learn.

It's also worth mentioning that if you are not a player and just want to focus on one woman for a relationship, this book will still be enormously helpful for you. The principles of texting remain the same.

Let us wait no longer. Stand up, go forth, and rise above the rest. It's time to begin!

Preamble

What messaging applications should I use?

WITH THE INVENTION OF THE SMART phone and mobile internet, the modern man has a wealth of options to choose from when it comes to messaging apps. Gone are the days when you would send a traditional text message (SMS) and hope it got to your recipient. Internet powered messaging apps are the most widely used globally and at Team Thorpe we recommend a few. WhatsApp has over 2 billion users in 180 countries and is arguably the most used messaging app. It has many advantages over SMS, however, the key advantage for the travelling man is that you can text women from different countries for free. You can also send photos, images, and audio, and you receive all kinds of other information from the app such as read receipts and profile photos from your contacts. Alternatives to WhatsApp are Telegram and Signal which offer almost identical functionality. If you are visiting the Balkans region and some parts of Eastern Europe, Viber is the most commonly used app.

For our Asian and Chinese cousins, WeChat is the go-to messaging app, possessing over 1 billion users. Facebook messenger also must get a mention. This is a backup, if for whatever reason WhatsApp is not an option when texting a woman. However, when meeting women, always ask if they have WhatsApp or your preferred messaging app before you take their number. This will guide you in collecting her number correctly. Wherever you are in the world, most people tend to hold onto their country of origin phone number so that they can stay in touch with people from home and message for free in the country they are staying in. When you are entering her number into your contacts book make sure you put + then the country code, then the phone number minus the first zero. During this moment, you can clarify with her that you have got the country code correct. If she's a native to the country you are in still type in the +, then the country code, then her phone number, especially if you are travelling and using a foreign number. Applying this rigorous approach ensures the number will work every time without fail. Then, when standing next to her, search for her in the messaging app and send her a quick message to check it works. The most common problem for the number not working after you have collected it is that you haven't added the + or the country code.

If you are staying more than a few weeks in a country, you could purchase a local SIM card and use that. The advantage here is you have a local number, so sending SMS's or making phone calls will be much cheaper, plus you can still use messaging apps. You also don't need to bother with entering international dialling prefixes. Having a local number also gives off the impression you are more of a permanent resident to a country rather than a travelling tourist.

To set yourself up correctly on these messaging apps, make sure you upload the best profile photo you can find. If you are not a good-looking man, don't worry, your profile photo should showcase your excellent dress sense and maybe show you standing next to a landmark or an instantly recognisable place. If you are reasonably attractive or better, let's get a close-up photo of you, you good-looking rooster! I recommend turning read receipts on because it shows you have nothing to hide when it comes to communicating with women and is also useful when practising some of the techniques in this book.

Now that you are all set up, let's take you on your journey to texting stardom!

Copy and Paste Zones

Use my texts

THROUGHOUT THE CHAPTERS YOU WILL see the following Copy and Paste Zones.

Copy & Paste Zone

Copy my text 1

Copy my text 2

Copy my text 3

These zones are for you to see exactly what I write at each stage of texting and for you to copy my lines and type them into your own text message conversations with women. Just make sure to change the name to the girl you are texting and remove my name at the end 😊. If you want to challenge yourself and learn even more, see what I provide in the Copy and Paste Zone and then craft your own message based on the principle I am teaching. Good luck!

1. The Texting Ladder

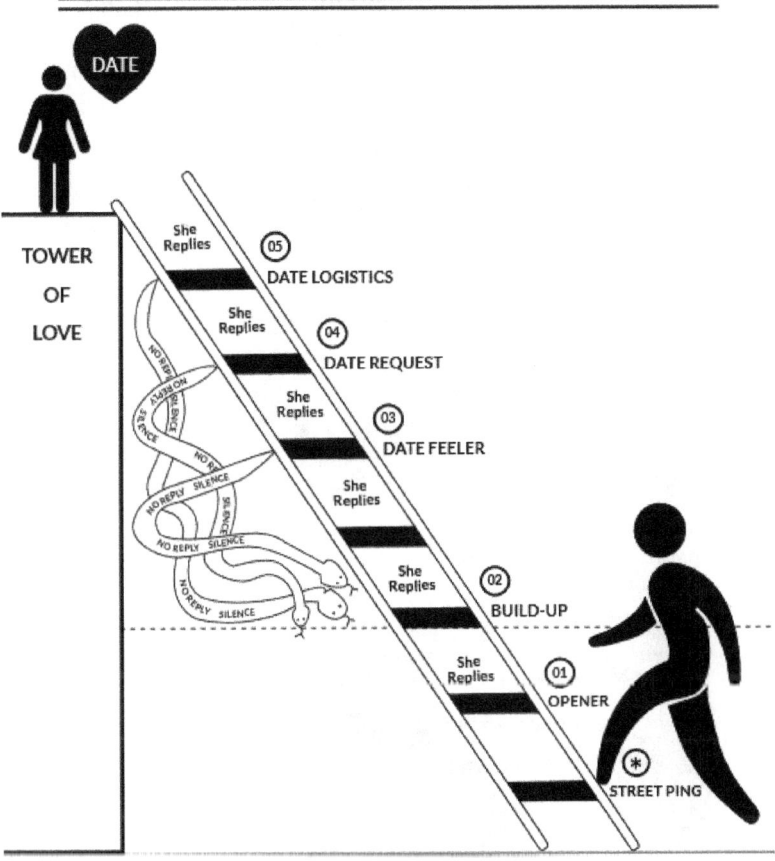

Figure 2. The Texting Ladder

ALL TEXT MESSSAGE INTERACTIONS WITH women should follow this basic structure.

After getting her number, you will go through a sequence of steps to get her out on a date.

Every time you text, and she replies, you take a step up on the ladder. If she doesn't reply to your text after a few days, you fall back to Step 2. If she doesn't agree to your date request, you fall back to Step 2. Follow the Texting Ladder process until you have booked in a date. You have reached your objective.

Here's an example:

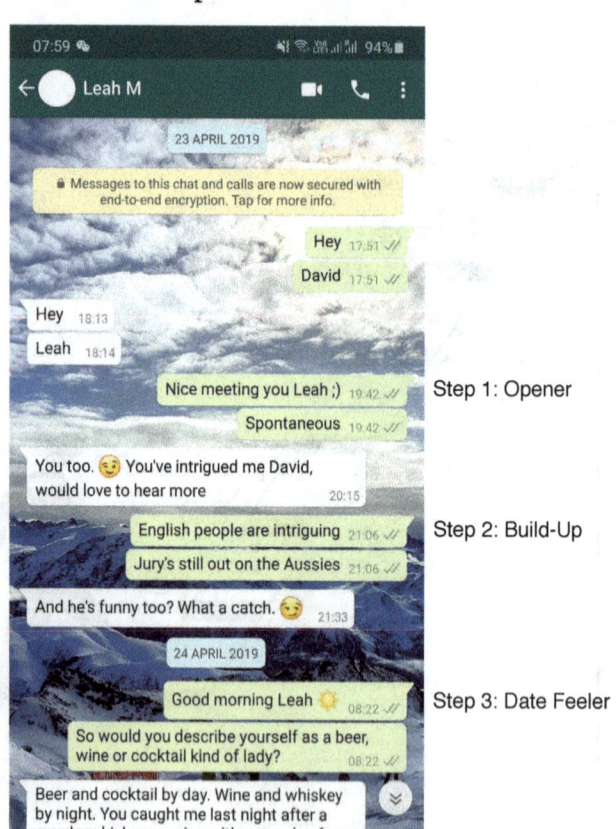

Step 1: Opener

This is something simple, a feeler. It should start the conversation, acknowledging your meeting and that's about it. Send the opener between one to three hours after meeting her. You can use call-back humour from your interaction in the opener to make it more personal or simply use her name. Call-back humour is where you refer back to a funny conversation topic you spoke about with her, such as what she was wearing when you met or an amusing story that she told you about. Don't ask questions. As you can see in the example, a simple "*Nice meeting you*" and "*Spontaneous*" has sufficed. Here are my other openers I use:

> **Copy & Paste Zone**
>
> Hey (woman's name), it was fun meeting you 😉 David
>
> Hey (woman's name), good to meet you. Spontaneous. David
>
> So, this must be the cheeky (insert nationality/dress/persona here) girl I met earlier. David
>
> Hi (woman's name), good to meet. You seem friendly. David
>
> Miss (woman's name) hello. It was spontaneous meeting you. David

The point of the opener is to start the text conversation and ultimately probe for investment. If she's even vaguely interested, she'll reply. You have taken your first step on the Texting Ladder.

Step 2: Build-Up

Now that you've laid the foundation for a conversation, it's time to build it up. The next one to two texts need to be simple and there are a few slightly different routes you can take. The purpose of these messages is to build up a conversation and show that you're not the kind of guy to dive straight into the date request and thus show neediness. In these messages you need to demonstrate that you are an interesting guy and have a cool life. Making statements about fun things you are doing, achievements, or inspirations will serve you well. You could also throw in an assumption or a tease out of something she told you when you met her to be a bit playful and light-hearted, which might spark a reaction. The canvas is yours to paint. There's no harm in a little exaggeration, sell it. Over these messages you will both show each other a little bit of personality.

Once she's replied to your opener you could say something like the following:

Copy & Paste Zone

> Just got home and preparing for my big speech tomorrow.

> I'm cooking a king prawn linguine. Being coached through it by Jamie Oliver.

> I'm off to my best friend's gig later. How about you?

> It's only 6pm but I bet (insert woman's name) is already in her pink pyjamas watching Netflix 😉

> On my way to work and ready to take on the world. Then will hit the gym after. How about you?

> Just delivered on my biggest project deadline. Win! Going out to celebrate with my team. How's your evening going?

You could use these exact messages or, better yet, tailor them to your own life. Every time she replies, look at how much she is writing. If she is giving one word or very curt answers, her investment levels are probably low. If she's writing a lot and asking multiple questions, she's very interested. You can ask questions in this step on the Texting Ladder but try to avoid it if you can when learning this step. If you do ask a question, make sure you've got your interesting statement out first. As long as she replies, you take another step up the Texting Ladder.

Step 3: Date Feeler

Once you've had a bit of texting after the opener it's time for the date feeler. This is a leading text to gently introduce the idea that you'll be asking her out. It increases the chance she'll say yes to the date request because she knew it was coming and it warms her up to the idea. It also builds up anticipation and creates a little tension on her side. In the example I write "*So would you describe yourself as a beer, wine or cocktail kind of lady?*" This is making it clear that a date request is coming and offers the opportunity for her to play into my frame and tell me her favourite drinks. Other examples of a date feeler could be:

> **Copy & Paste Zone**
>
> So, would you describe yourself as a beer, wine or cocktail kind of lady?
>
> What are you doing on (insert day)?
>
> When it comes to wine are you red or white, dry or sweet?
>
> Do you prefer cafes or bars for fun?
>
> If we were drinking a cocktail which one would you be choosing...? You can always tell a lot about a girl by analysing her poison of choice ;-)
>
> Have you been to (insert your city) best new bar?

If she responds positively you've taken a step up to the date request. If she responds but not as you would have hoped, for example, *"I don't drink"* then you are still at the date feeler step. You need to reframe and have another go. In the example of not being a drinker, you could go with *"Hmm a sensible lady indeed. Coffee it is."* If she replies positively, or simply acknowledges this then you've taken a step up and it's time for the date request.

Step 4: Date Request

Now that you've prepared the ground for the date, it's time to ask her out. In the example above, I write *"Let's go for a drink. Friday after work or Sunday afternoon."* This is an assertive request, offering a time that is suitable for me and will hopefully be good for her. You don't want to appear too available and you are hoping that she will be free when you are. If she's into you she'll go for it. Notice I didn't ask her a question. I simply stated we should go for a drink and here is my availability. Sundays through to Thursdays are a good time to have dates because these are the days people generally have more free time. Fridays and Saturdays are prime time days when people are likely to be busy, however, you can still propose a date on these days if the connection between you is strong and you feel she is likely to accept your request. You can ask her out through a question but when learning this step try and use assertive statements to build your confidence over text. Here's some date requests I use:

Copy & Paste Zone

Let's meet for a drink. I'm free Tuesday evening or Thursday evening.

Let's go for that drink. I can do Monday evening or Saturday afternoon. How about you?

How about we grab a coffee on Saturday morning or Sunday morning. My shout.

Let's head to (your cities local landmark) and take in the views. Can you do Wednesday evening or Thursday evening?

This step needs careful management and if you get it wrong you can lose her entirely. If you make the date request and she declines your proposal but offers an alternative then it is fine to make another date request when she is free, assuming you are. This is the only time you can make a second date request. If she refuses you outright and gives no alternatives, you have climbed as far as you can on the Texting Ladder. And just like the game Snakes and Ladders, it's time to slide down Mr Thorpe's dirty big snake, back to Step 2. To the unlearned and desperate man, if his first date request is refused, he'll simply ask her out a second, third, and maybe even a fourth time in the hope that his badgering beats her into submission. It won't, and he'll be blocked or archived as she realises he is needy and desperate. Make sure this isn't you.

If your date request has been rejected and you've returned to the humble heights of Step 2 on the Texting Ladder, do not despair. Leave the text conversation alone for a day or two and then resume your climb back up the Texting Ladder. You may have just got unlucky on the first date request with her being out of town or having an exceptional circumstance, e.g. family birthday. In this case, building the text conversation back up again will be no problem and she'll accept your second date request. If you've climbed up the Texting Ladder multiple times and asked her out and she's declined all of your requests, she's not interested and it's time to move on.

Step 5: Date Logistics
With the hard work done, this step is confirming the arrangements for the date which is simply the day, the

time, and the place to meet. In the example, I propose a sensible after work time for a Friday and a central, well-known location in my city. From this location it is a nice walk to the first bar. Keep this step simple and straightforward and you won't go far wrong. If she can't make your proposed time or doesn't know where your meeting place is, demonstrate some flexibility in the texting; changing the time or place, or both, to make sure you get the date booked in. Here are some examples:

Copy & Paste Zone

Great. Let's meet at the square at Central, 6pm Thursday.

Cool. I'll meet you outside the bar, 5:30pm.

See you next to the big clock by the pond. 6pm Wednesday.

Texting the time and place to her suggests you have a plan. Women want men to lead and when it comes to dating, they certainly want you to have a plan. After all, you invited her out. This is another way you can demonstrate a strong masculine frame that will transition nicely from texting to dating. More on frame later.

If you're reading this and are thinking "great, but I have no idea how to plan a date or what to do on a date" then I suggest you visit my website where you can learn everything you need to know at succeeding at dating.

This comprehensive tutorial will teach you everything you need to know about dating.

SUMMARY

So, there you have it, the Texting Ladder. Of course, there are endless varieties as to how a texting conversation will actually play out, but the principles of the Texting Ladder remain the same. When you follow the structure, you are initiating and building up the conversation over a series of texts that leads naturally to a date request. It also shows you're not needy by not diving in and asking her out straight away.

When texting, observe her actions and not her words. How long is she taking to reply and how much is she writing? These are key indicators of her interest levels and investment in you. When starting out with this, all of your texts should aim to add value which means making her laugh, smile, or at the very least triggering a slight emotional response. That can either be through what is communicated or how it is communicated.

Remember, this is your conversation to lead, so lead it. This is what we call frame. There are many dating and lifestyle books entirely dedicated to frame and frame control so it can be a deep, complex topic. However, all you need to know is whoever is leading and steering the conversation has the frame. This is a good thing, and you want to have the frame. To put it another way, frame is like you being the owner of a shop. You arrange the shop how you want it and fill the shop with products of your choice. This is your frame, it is your reality. Customers then come into your shop, experience it, and buy your products. The customers are the women. It is their shopping experience, but you orchestrated it and lead it. In support of your frame you should adopt the mentality that you want her, but you don't need her. There is just enough energy from your side to progress the conversation up the Texting Ladder, but it's not critical that you do so. To learn more about frame in all aspects of life, I recommend a book called "Pitch Anything" by Oren Klaff.

Texting should be simple and, as we said in the beginning, it is a means to get a woman out on a date. Nothing more. Follow this structure and you will start going out on dates. You don't need to tell her your life story and you don't need to write an elaborate novel on male-female dynamics. You just need to do the bare minimum to advance the conversation on.

However, you and I know that things will not always be so easy. Not every conversation you have will go seamlessly. There will be problems, there will be anomalies, there will be reactions and there will be things she does that you don't understand, and which will be downright frustrating. But that's what the rest of this book is for: to teach you the other tools and techniques you need to become a well-rounded texter, so you run into less problems and increase your chances of hearing "Yes" when you ask a woman out. Finally, I have a troubleshooting chapter that details the most common problems you'll experience and how to solve them.

2. Easy things you can do to win at Texting

"I can do it with my eyes shut!"

HERE ARE SOME EASY TO understand housekeeping tips to improve your texting alongside using the Texting Ladder.

2. 1. Say my name say my name!

Destiny's Child sang it so it must be right! People respond much better to others when their name is used in any type of conversation. It wakes them up, makes it personal and is a sign of respect. Simply referencing the name of the woman you are texting in messages makes it more personal and direct. I also encourage you to do this because if you are a bit of a lady killer and are talking to lots of women, there will be the temptation to send them all the same message such as a ping text (we'll cover pinging and broadcasting later). Whilst mass transmission of a message may work for some women, others will already have a good feel for the kind of bad boy you are and you may get a negative reaction or resistance to your texting conversation from these women. *"I bet you say that to all the girls"* or

"*How many girls did that message go to?*" will certainly ring true from these women. Now that's not to say you can't send the same message to the women you are texting, just personalise it more by using her name and tailor it a bit to the texting conversation you are having with her. Doing this will take more time, but your texting conversations will be more personal and receive less drama.

Another naming technique you can practise is giving the woman you are texting a nickname. This can be literally anything you want and ideally is sourced from the interaction you had with the woman when you met her. For example, if you were teasing her in the bar and said she looked like a chipmunk, the name chipmunk could reappear in the texting conversation. You'll certainly get a reaction from it and, if she likes it, it makes your texting conversation a bit more fun and colourful. It also makes the conversation unique and stands out against the other guys she'll be texting as only you two will share this new identity of hers. You may find she gives you a nickname and a fun texting conversation follows! Here's an example:

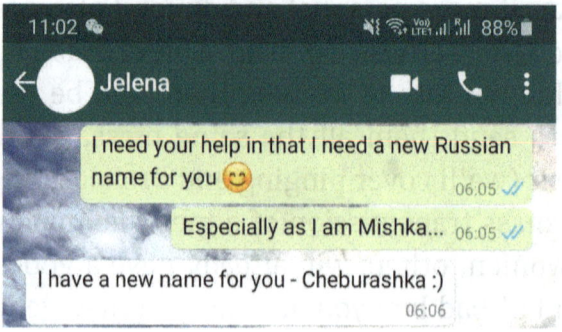

Nicknames are another form of framing. You are branding her in a fun way with a cute or mischievous name and she plays along with it. If she doesn't like the nickname and is not willing to play along with finding a new one, just drop it and stick to using her real name.

Nicknames also need to be congruent with the interaction you had together. A universal go to nickname is "trouble" or "cheeky." However, if, for example, there is nothing trouble or cheeky about the woman you met and she's as straight laced as the village librarian, branding her as "trouble" or "cheeky" will come out of nowhere for her and may come across as a bit strange. This is because it's not congruent with your interaction and your texting up until this point. So, before you send a nickname, ask yourself, is she really trouble? Or, is she really like that cute animal, for example?

Nicknames are not essential, and you can do very well in texting without ever having to use them. However, they are worth deploying every now and then and some women will love them, which makes texting a lot more fun and enjoyable.

2. 2.   Write like Shakespeare, not like Trump...

"If texting be the food of love, play on!" Not quite, but you get the message. Another quick win to bring your texting up to par is to write correctly in your language. The correct use of grammar and punctuation should be applied. Abbreviations and short-hand texting such as "*c u l8r*" should not be used. Thankfully, with the invention of smart phones and full-sized QWERTY keyboards the days of texting like an urban gangster are over. However, if you do indulge in a bit of post millennial texting, stop it. It's an outdated look and there's no reason to write like this. You also want to appear like a well-educated man to the women you are texting.

The introduction of the smart phone also brought with it the emoji. The use of emojis should be kept to a minimum. I'm sure we've all seen people in impassioned debate with their friends as to whether they should send a happy or a winky smiley to someone they fancy. Emojis can add a bit of colour and fun to a texting conversation, but don't overdo it; you don't want to be known as one of those people who send unicorns, sausages, and umbrellas in every bloody message. They don't make much difference and, if you overuse them, you'll be branded as a weirdo.

Neither should BLOCK CAPITALS be used under any circumstances; she'll think you escaped from an asylum.

Another common mistake is texting on the move and not thinking. We're all guilty of it in our 21st century lives; walking, talking, and texting, head down in a busy street whilst also thinking about work, family, and friends. That's a lot of distractions, especially when you can get blown out by an attractive, high value woman from one bad text. Here's an example:

There's no reason for me to send this image of a forest hut. I just finished a successful first date with this girl and there's nothing more for me to say after she writes *"I certainly do"*. However, 20 minutes later I'm back out with friends, changing bars, walking and talking and thinking I can be funny, send this catastrophe of a text. She either misconstrues what I'm getting at or doesn't like my joke and takes it badly. This was the end of the conversation and any chance of a second date. If you're reading this book, texting means something to you and it means not messing it up. Avoid distracting environments and doing too many things at once when texting. Wait until you are home or in a quiet environment where you can think, read the texting stream, and craft your message.

2. 3. Paralysis analysis – the use of notes

When you first start out learning all of this, a very common fear guys have is making a mistake and not really knowing what to text. They fill the message bubble with their message, then 5 seconds later doubt themselves and rewrite it. Then rewrite it some more. Other times, guys will write what they think is a good text, send it, then regret it later and bemoan with, "What was I thinking?!" You need to recognise that in these scenarios your mind is reactive and needs to be calmed.

To avoid this, use the notes app on your phone. Create a new note and write your text in there as a draft and see how it looks and feels. Edit it as much as you like and, if you are still not sure, save it and leave it for a while. After a few hours, come back to it and reflect upon it. It's amazing what your subconscious mind can do for you, processing away to see if you are comfortable to send that message or not. The other advantage of using notes is exactly that: you are not in the actual messaging app where one false touch of the screen could send your message! Not only can you use your notes as a whiteboard for texting debauchery, you can build one note up into a template of all your favourite texting openers, phrases, and go-to date requests. Then, when you need to, you can copy and paste your preferred message, tailor it a little with her name, and send it. Easy!

2. 4.   Ellipsis...

Using... at the end of your messages is a great way to build up some tension and trigger some anticipation for the woman. It means there's more to say, more to discover...

Just about anything can be suggested and it leaves her mind to fill in the rest. Of course, the use of ellipsis does need to be moderated otherwise she'll think you're struggling with a brain injury if you use it after every single message. The times when ellipsis are most effective is during flirting or when the texting is hotting up and escalating. Here's an example:

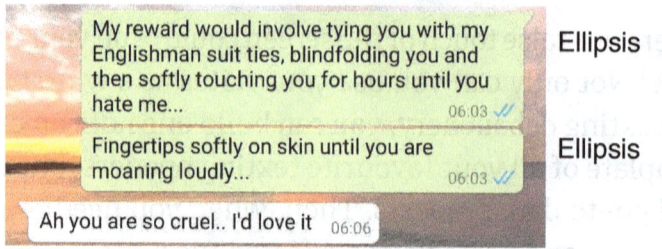

2. 5. Ask less questions

If you're a texting newbie, one of the most effective things you can do to improve is to ask less questions. The uninitiated guy will worry that if they don't ask a question at the end of every message she won't reply and all will be lost. Not so.

Simply asking less questions in your messages and, instead, making assertive statements and telling her all of the interesting things that you are up to will make a big difference. Imagine if you were texting President Obama. He's not going to be asking you how your day is every 5 minutes. He's a high value alpha male who makes assertions and statements and drives the frame. It's his conversation; come, join in. Make it your new challenge to see how many messages you can go up the Texting Ladder without asking a question. Here's an example:

I'm halfway up the Texting Ladder and I didn't ask a single question! A few days later I get her out on a date.

Now that's not to say you should never ask questions. You should. Just less. And when you do make it an open question that she can really respond to and invest in. Some examples could be asking about her future aspirations or finding out she's been sick recently and asking her how she's feeling. Then, once she's given you a good topic to explore, stick to the topic and text about that for a few messages. This is what we call ploughing and shows you are interested in what she has to say, while also demonstrating social intelligence. You could ask these types of questions in the build-up phase of the Texting Ladder.

2. 6.   What time is it Mr Thorpe?

Another area you can conquer quickly is the time of day you are texting. There are day-time and night-time texting windows you need to be aware of that you must work within. For the day-time, don't text too early, like 5am or 6am. If you are an early riser, she may not be, and she may not turn her phone off at night which could disturb her and wake her up if you text her. The time before work can be an effective window to send a text because she is most probably commuting like you and has some time for her phone. In work time, I do not recommend texting your leads, except maybe at lunchtime. Think about it, what message does that send about you? Are you one of those people who doesn't take their profession seriously and is messing about on their phone all day? It's not what high value men do; they take their work seriously. Being unavailable because of your work is a good thing, so don't text during this time. The evening is the largest window of opportunity to text. From after work you have until around 10:30pm on a weeknight. Between 8:00pm – 10:30pm is usually the most active time window for women because, like the rest of the population, they're probably sat on the sofa after dinner, chilling with their phone. Do not text after 11:00pm or into the early hours on a weekend. It gives the impression you're a bit strange and not cognisant of the fact that most people are sleeping at this time. Again, you could disturb her if she hasn't turned her phone off.

Beyond this, also recognise a larger time window and that is, how long she will be texting you and potentially meeting up with you since you got her number. Imagine a fully open window. This is the moment when you get the number and your texting relationship begins. Over time, the window slowly closes until it is closed, and the lead is dead. The window of opportunity is always closing, no matter what is going on over texting. This means you need to text your leads and get them out on dates otherwise they will go cold. Furthermore, it means you need to work your way up the Texting Ladder, ideally over the first few days, so that you can get to that all-important date request and get her booked in. If you can do this within the first week, great!

From experience, if you haven't got her out on a date after about 2 weeks since collecting the number your chances of doing so beyond this time window are slim. It also communicates that, despite your best efforts, she is not interested.

For women who you are going on dates with or who you have started relationships with, your window of opportunity is closing much more slowly. Providing you are keeping in touch and seeing them in person, the window won't close on you.

2. 7. Go fast or go slow? Mirroring and Crescendos

This is probably one of the most important chapters in this book. Get this right and you'll seriously improve your texting abilities with women. In this chapter we'll cover mirroring, which is reflecting her energy over text. We'll also cover crescendos, where the energy in the conversation peaks. Let's start with mirroring.

When you get the number and begin texting a woman, you can learn a huge amount about how interested she is in you and the kind of texter she is. You can deduce these things from how fast she is texting you back and how long her responses are. The perfect scenario for any man is that after you send the opener she replies almost immediately, writes a lot, and shows high levels of investment and enthusiasm. If this happens to you, smile, and bask in texting glory! However, you now need to manage this hot potato correctly. Guys who are starting out on their texting journey may well experience this but think that it's cool and high-value to leave it a few hours or to reply the following day. Are you mad?! You have a woman who is seriously interested in you! What you need to do is mirror her energy. You don't do this by laying on the compliments or writing lots back, but by advancing up the Texting Ladder quickly and efficiently. Recognise that you could get her booked in for a date the same day you met her, over text. Here's an example:

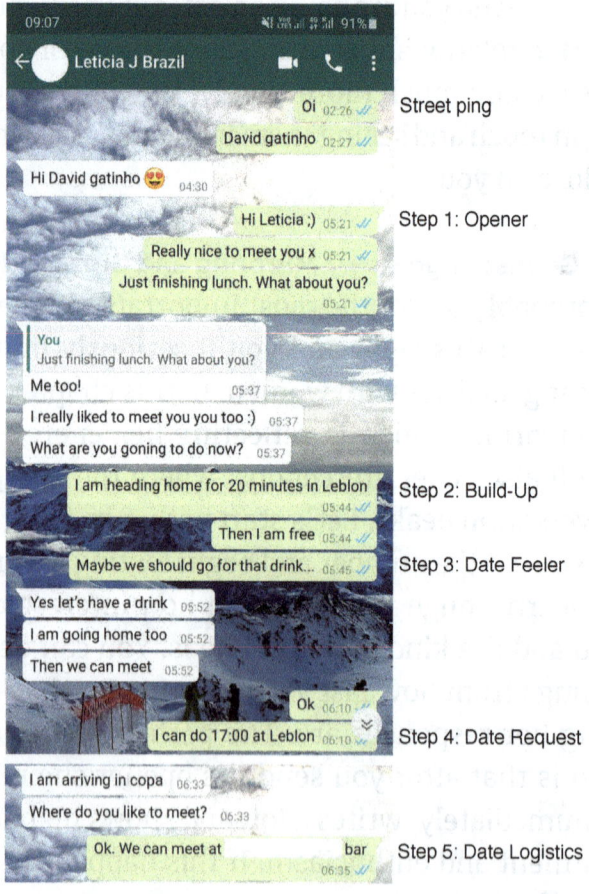

Easy things you can do to win at Texting

Within a few hours of the opener, a date is secured. You can see on the time stamps that she is replying within minutes. I recognise from my interaction with her on the street and over text that she is keen and I also recognise the fast replies she is giving. I am now calibrated to the situation and mirror her energy by also replying within minutes. My objective is to seize this opportunity and climb up the Texting Ladder as fast as I can and get her booked in for a date. You will notice that I slightly cheat the rules of the Texting Ladder by sending the build-up message and the date feeler together; this is a low risk move considering her high investment levels. Within twenty minutes of the text stream beginning with the opener, I am seeding the date, and within fifty minutes from the opener I am making the date request and we are talking date logistics. Two hours later, the date is booked in. And one hour after this we meet up on our date.

Mirroring and reflecting her energy is another key step in your journey to improve your texting. If she's showing lots of interest and texting back fast, return the energy in kind and feed the fire. If she's a slow, considered texter, mirror that pace and energy level. Doing this just makes the conversation more natural and ensures neither of you are out of sync with one another. Do keep in mind that the same woman can be both a fast and a slow texter, it just depends what's going on for her and her emotional connection with you. Again, like the shape-shifter you are, respond to these fast bursts of texting, and then ease off for the slower, more relaxed pacing of messaging. For the slower texting women you are managing, do keep one eye on that texting window we talked about earlier. If you both go too slow, that window will start closing and her interest in you will fade away. If this does start to happen, you'll need to reply a bit faster than she is doing to move yourself up the Texting Ladder and get that date booked in. It is a fine balance between pushing the speed agenda before the window closes and appearing needy and pushing her away.

Another vital aspect of texting to watch out for is when the texting has hit a crescendo, or, no pun intended, a climax. Here, the texting conversation experiences a surge in positive energy and a peak is reached. This is the perfect opportunity to go for the date request; when she's invested in you and happy with the conversation. Here's an example:

Positive surge begins

Leave it for the night

The background to this conversation is prior to these screenshots the texting was quite straightforward and a bit boring; not much was happening. Then, where you can see her saying I can read her mind, the conversation picks up. Either she was just feeling keen in that moment or my prior text prompted a reaction. It doesn't really matter. The texting pace and volume from her side takes off suddenly and she shows a lot of investment in her compliments and in the amount she is writing. However, as the conversation progresses you can see from the timings that it's getting quite late and I had a choice to make: ask her out when it's late and she's potentially signed off for the evening, or keep it cool, leave it and ask her out the following morning. I opt for the latter which works. We've built enough of a relationship together over text for the crescendo to still be there the following morning. The rest of the texting is basic logistics. If the crescendo had started earlier in the day, then yes, the date request would have come on the same day.

So, the next time you're texting and it starts to go really well and the energy picks up, prepare yourself for racing up the Texting Ladder and sending that date request. You'll increase your chances significantly when you're asking her out on a high. And as you get better with texting, you can start to manoeuvre conversations towards crescendos. We'll talk about this more in the Push-Pull chapter and sparking a reaction.

However, some conversations don't experience such spikes of interest, even with your best efforts. You don't need crescendos in order to climb up the Texting Ladder, and as long as you are progressing and you get her out, the conversation can be as boring as two nuns sex texting each other. Think of crescendos as a nice added extra. Enjoy them when they happen, but don't worry if they don't.

3. In the beginning, there was the street ping...

"In the beginning God created the heavens and...texting."

YOU MAY HAVE NOTICED IN my earlier screenshots of conversations that there were a few preliminary messages between the woman and I before the opener. These messages were sent when we actually met; on the street or in a bar. As you've probably realised, at Team Thorpe we don't really do internet dating; we prefer a face-to-face approach. It's more authentic, real, and masculine to meet women in this way. If you want to learn more about how to succeed at approaching women in real life - on the street, in bars or in fact anywhere but your internet dating app - head over to my website where you can learn everything you need to know about approaching like a boss..

www.davidthorpedating.com

Now, let's explore why we would begin texting a woman when we are standing next to them. First of all, it proves that the number she's given us actually works. Any guy who meets women face-to-face will have at least one story to tell where they got the number of their dream girl but typed in the number to their contacts book incorrectly, or she made a mistake giving the number and they walked away; the communications link broken forever. Gutted!

And then, in the post 2010 era, we had internet powered texting apps, such as WhatsApp and Telegram, which meant people could keep their country of origin phone number and text anyone they wanted to. This meant all kinds of confusion for the approaching man, now he had to get the country code correct, make sure there's a +, drop the first zero or forget all of that and try and stick with a normal text message which may or may not work. All of these problems are still very much present and what you do not want is for the hard work of the approach, the conversation, and the number close to amount to nothing. It's such a basic thing to get right at the end of your conversation and yet we are all susceptible of making one small mistake at the end and losing her forever.

So, to prevent all of this from happening and to make sure you have a phone number that actually works, we begin texting whilst still in the interaction. When she has agreed to give you her phone number, you need to know which texting app you'll be using. For me, it's nearly always WhatsApp. I ask her if she has WhatsApp when taking her number. Most women these days say yes. Whether you type in her number or she does, when

you're done, make sure you edit it there and then by deleting the first zero and replacing with a + then the country code. Let's look at a UK example:
  She enters her number as: 01234567891
  You edit it to: +441234567891 where 44 is the UK international prefix.
  If she or you is pressed for time, you could quickly type in her number and call her. Once you see your number on her screen, cancel the call. Edit the number with the + and the country prefix after the interaction.
  Once you've saved her number into your phone, open your preferred texting app and search for her. It may take a minute for the texting app to find her, but she should appear. If her number doesn't immediately appear, keep her talking. If after a few minutes she's still not appearing, you have an issue with her number which you need to figure out. Be pleased you caught the problem now and not later! However, once you've found her, quickly write a *"Hey"* or *"Hi trouble"* and hit send. Doing this in front of her and telling her what you're doing should compel her to get her phone out to see if she received the message. If she stands there and doesn't get her phone out, simply ask her if it worked. She should get her phone out to see if she received your message. Often throwing in a tease on this first message can get a little giggle from her who may there and then write you a cheeky message back. Nice! Knowing that she received your message is a great confidence boost for you at the end of the conversation because you know you have a working communications link between the two of you. No more worrying about if you got the number wrong. Another tip is, after the

interaction, update her name in your contacts book by adding a few details about her so you can remember her more easily later, especially if you pick up a few numbers on that day. For example, "Laura" could be "Laura Lawyer" or "Laura Red Coat." Adding a few details will serve you well to trigger your memory later on and give you some good cues to refer to in your texting conversation.

Another tip you can implement is if you are regularly approaching and getting multiple numbers per session, add the date in the company field of the contact. Something like '24Jan23' for all the contacts you got that day. Then, later on when you are texting your leads you can go to your contacts book and type in the search bar '24Jan23' and all the numbers you collected that day will appear. Magic!

As you can see, adopting this multifaceted approach to number collection is very direct and disciplined, ensuring you obtain her number correctly every single time. However, your direct, assertive approach will also flush out women who are not interested. One technique women can employ on you if they are not interested is to give you a fake number. However, your disciplined approach to number collection will show her there is no getting past you. When she realises this, she may raise an objection and say she's not comfortable giving her number to you. If you can see she is being sincere and not playful when saying this, respect her decision and leave the interaction. Do not feel downbeat, the woman has saved you a lot of wasted texting time and you can quickly move on to finding a woman who is interested in you.

Secondly, there is another good reason why we send the first text when we are still talking to her. Once you've sent your first message, said your goodbyes, and left the interaction, an opportunity has been created for her to start texting you back first. You may find your phone starting to buzz with text message notifications after a few minutes...

If you had a good interaction with her, and she is interested and available she might not be able to resist texting you. After all, you're a cool guy who just came up to her, struck up a conversation, and asked her out there and then. Why wouldn't she want to talk with you? If she does start texting you, it's time to bask in texting glory! This is a great sign and shows she's really into you. Now you can pocket the achievement and carry on with your day or evening and text her later, or you could indulge and kick off the texting conversation straight away. Here's an example from a street interaction I had with one of the hottest girls I've ever met:

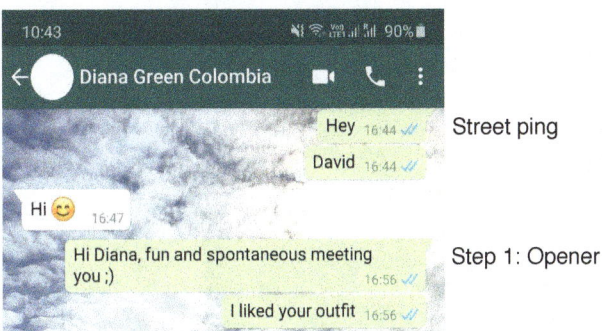

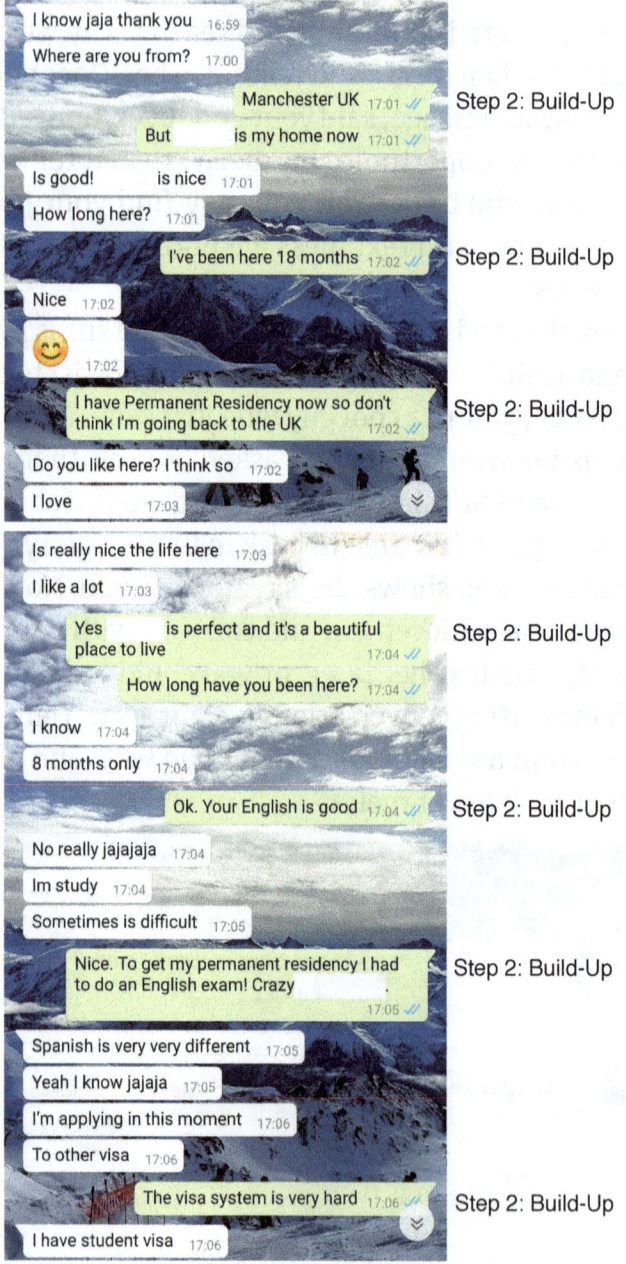

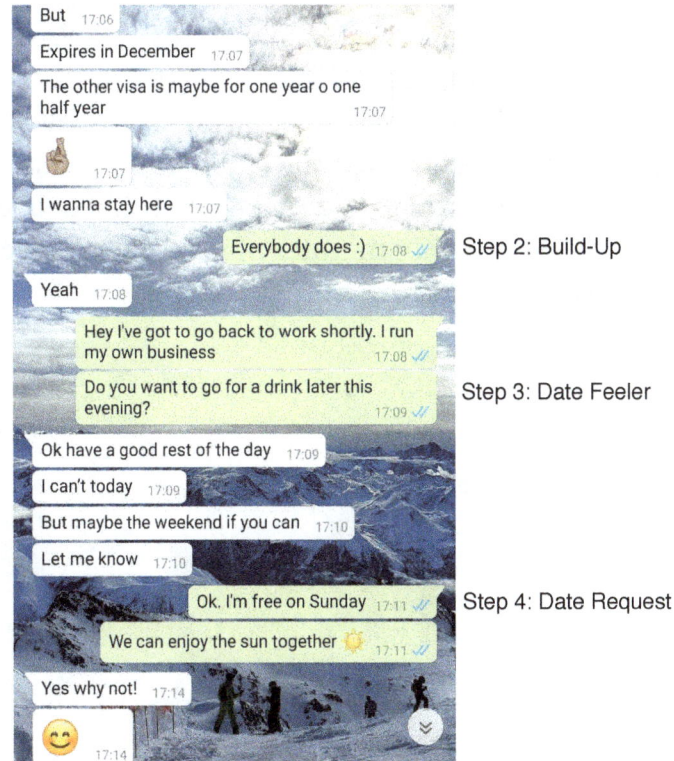

As soon as I'd sent, "*Hey*" and "*David*" and she showed me she'd received the message, we hugged, said goodbye and I walked away. Three minutes later, she replied. We must have only been one block apart in the city by this point, but a texting conversation had already begun. On this occasion and after a good interaction, I decided to carry on the conversation. Sticking to the Texting Ladder structure, we texted each other back and forth and her responses were almost instant. I didn't need to do anything special here except stay on topic and progress up the Texting Ladder to the date request. By allowing the conversation to flow naturally, I stayed at Step 2 in the build-up phase of the Texting Ladder for most of the text message stream and then transitioned to the date feeler and date request. Within 30 minutes of saying goodbye on the street I had a date booked in with this stunning girl. This is why you send that initial message in the interaction. First, it proves her number works, and second, you can deduce her interest levels within minutes of meeting and even book her in for a date.

4. Shit tests and how to pass them

"Answer me these questions three..."

BY NOW SOME OF THE women you are in conversation with are probably impressed with your texting abilities you have learned from the first few chapters of this book. They may even be thinking about going on that date with you. But if you think it's that straightforward you are mistaken. She's not just going to let you climb up the Texting Ladder unhindered. Oh no. It's time she threw a spanner in the works. It's time for shit tests.

Shit tests are a fascinating subject and a woman who is attracted to you will often start throwing these your way at any stage of the relationship; from the first 5 minutes to 5 years of marriage. What she is doing here is testing your value as a man. When women are attracted to men, they feel a strong emotional connection towards them. They have perceived that you have value as a man and they like it. However, to verify your value, they need to test that it's really there. It's a women's safety net and it is there for good reason. After all, they are responsible for the future of the human race, and they don't want to be spending their time with a con man.

Shit tests can come in many forms. They can be presented as malicious questions, personal attacks, or framing you in a derogatory way. You need to recognise when you are being shit tested and, more importantly, know what to do about them.

The first thing you must do is not react to a shit test. Recognise she is attracted to you and simply venting sexual tension. Don't take shit tests personally and be thankful for them; she considers you a viable sexual option. If a hot girl isn't sending shit tests, you are deep in the friend zone or, in very rare scenarios, she is totally into you and doesn't need to double check your value.

You can respond in one of several ways to shit tests. The best way is to not take a shit test seriously and thus, not acknowledge it. You simply sidestep it and carry on the texting conversation as if she never tested you. She's letting off some steam, so let her. Another way is to make a game of the shit test which shows that you don't care. Finally, for the really tough shit tests where she's crossed the line, all you need to do is calmly point out that she's overstepped the mark and move on. Deep down, the woman knows her shit tests are not to be taken seriously; she's just venting the sexual tension she's experiencing and hoping you can pick up on the message and manage the situation accordingly. Secretly, she wants you to win and pass the shit test successfully, because then you'll have proven that you have the value she thinks you possess.

Let's look at an example of not acknowledging a shit test and sidestepping it:

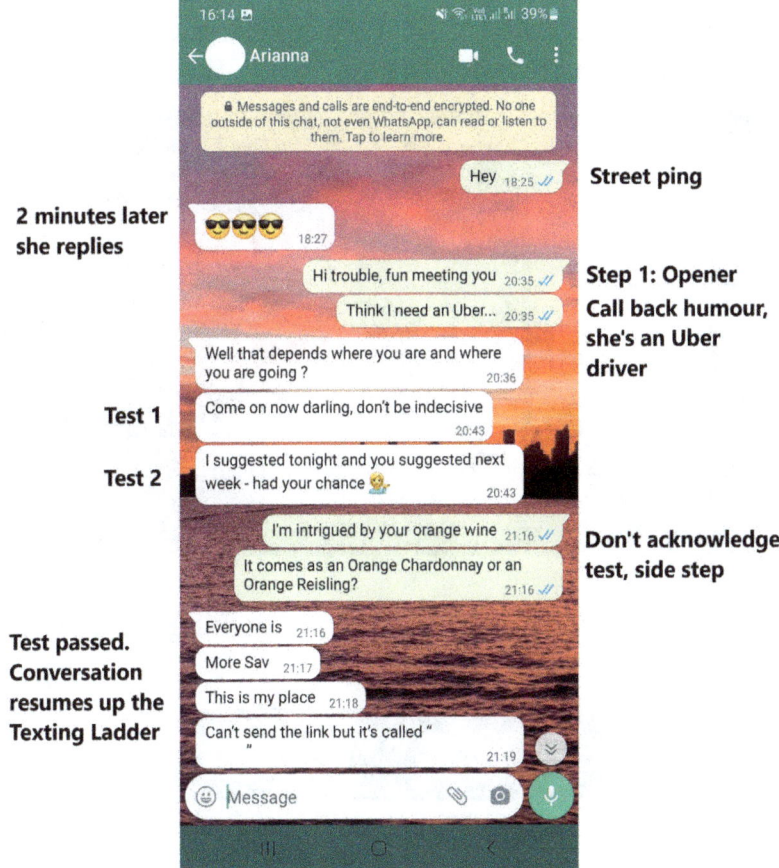

In this example, I don't acknowledge the shit test. I simply let it pass me by and bring in a conversation topic we talked about in depth on the street. The uninitiated man may have panicked, seeing that she was threatening to walk away forever with the "*had your chance*" message. However, a simple non-acknowledgement suffices and, in addition, I knew she was attracted to me because she replied to my text within 2 minutes of leaving the conversation. You can watch a video of me explaining this texting conversation on my YouTube Channel, video titled '<u>How To Pass Her Tests Over Text – Sidestep Technique With Screenshot Example</u>.'

Now let's look at an example of making a game of a shit test:

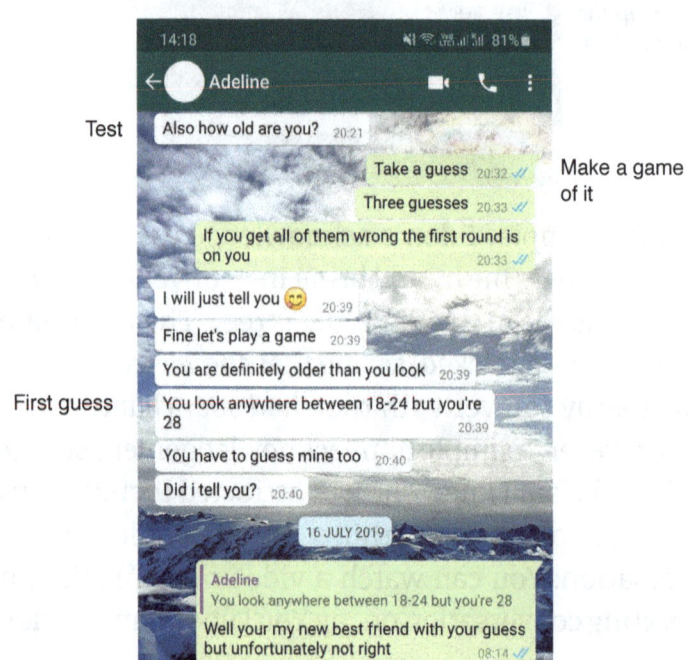

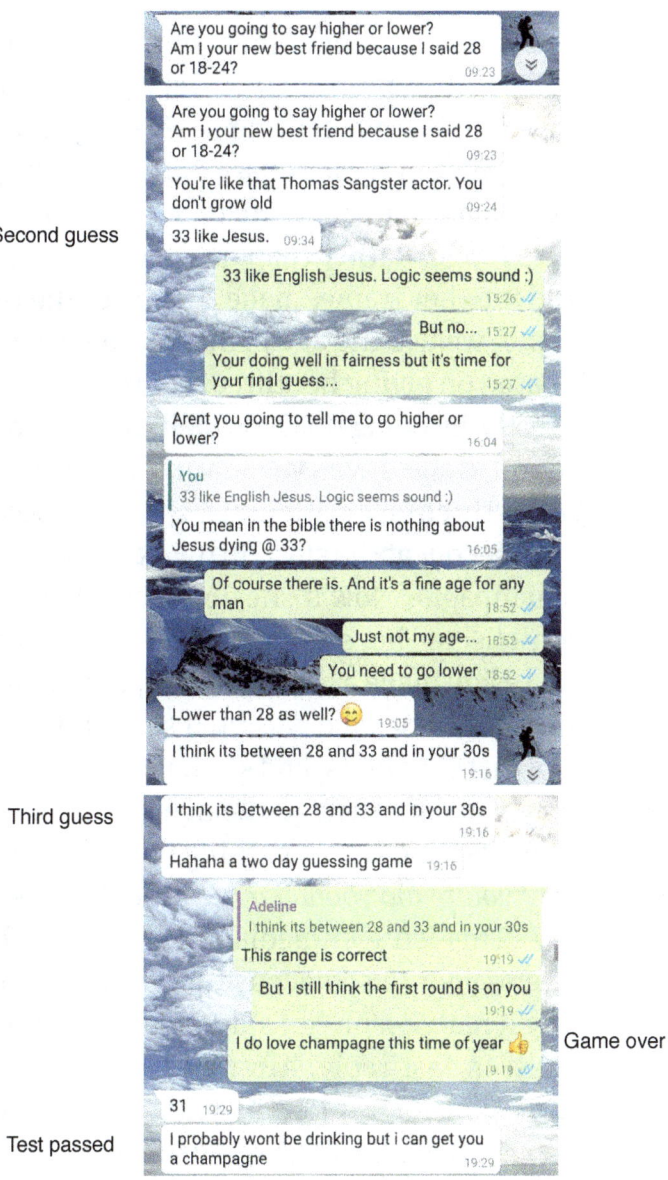

Being asked about your age is the most common shit test of them all. When this happens, the woman is screening you. She is attracted and has perceived you have value; now it needs to be tested. One way she can do this is by establishing your age and seeing if the answer is acceptable to her. The more attracted she is to you, the more willing she'll be to accepting a wider age range. Her value also comes into the equation. If she's a high-value, young woman, she can afford to be picky with her acceptable age range. Rather than answer her straight away and fold into her frame, make a game of the test. In this example, we use the age game. As you can see, the game is based on giving her three attempts to guess your age correctly. By doing this, you maintain your hold on the frame and, if she's even vaguely interested, she'll play along. After three failed attempts, she has to accept the penalty you set out at the start, in my example this is buying me champagne. Now if she does guess your age correctly, don't lie: tell her she got it right. You still pass the test because you made a game out of it, were honest when the moment came, she garnered some information about you that she wants, and she had to work for it.

Another way you can manage the age test is to give her a push over text and say something like, *"you're too old for me"* or *"you're too young for me"* and don't write anything else. This isn't immediately answering her question, asserts your mischievous frame and is a bold move, causing a reaction on her side which will almost certainly result in fast reply. After a bit of toing and froing you can then answer her question. More on the technique of pushing in the chapter Push Pull.

Now let's look at an example of where a woman crosses the line on a shit test:

Shit tests and how to pass them

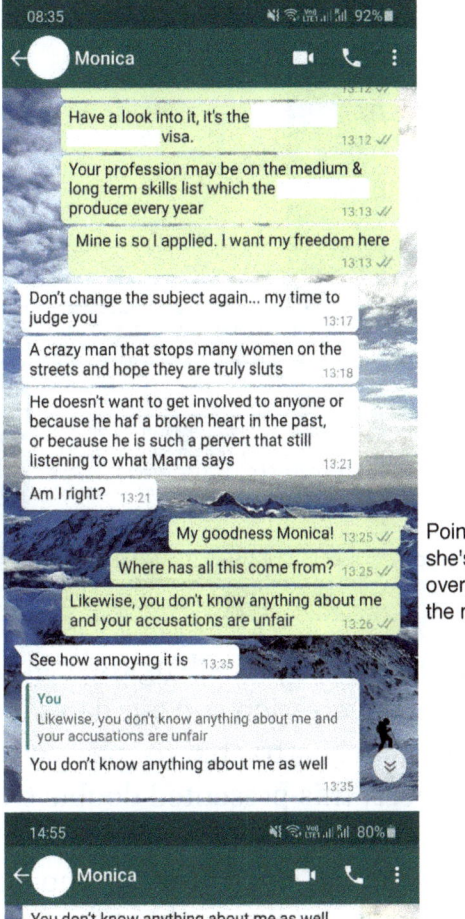

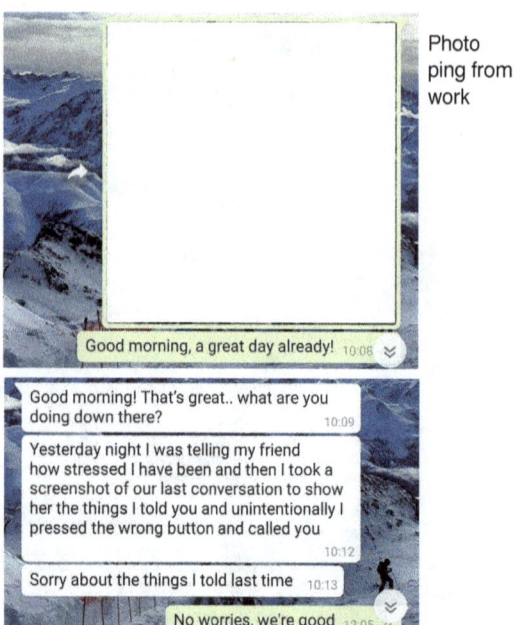

Photo ping from work

Good morning, a great day already! 10:08

Good morning! That's great.. what are you doing down there? 10:09

Yesterday night I was telling my friend how stressed I have been and then I took a screenshot of our last conversation to show her the things I told you and unintentionally I pressed the wrong button and called you 10:12

Test passed

Sorry about the things I told last time 10:13

No worries, we're good 12:05

Monica was indeed a challenging one! However, over the texting conversation and our dates it emerged that she was seriously attracted to me and that I was her type. However, this presented double trouble for her, hence the strength of her shit tests. Monica was a high-value, young, smart woman who dismissed most men she came into contact with. So, when I came to her attention a simple shit test wouldn't do. She wanted to test for the highest value and went all in to see if she could break my frame in one blow. My response came in two halves. First, I called her out on overstepping the mark and kept calm. In her response, she started to climb down but she was still on the warpath. The second half of my response came in vacuuming for two days. More on vacuuming later, but I went quiet for two whole days and she got zero attention from me. To fill the silence, she messaged me twice to probe if I was still there. However, I stayed quiet. I then send a standard photo ping not acknowledging her tirade of abuse where she then apologised, and the test was passed. The second half of my response punished her with the silent treatment and it was this that won the day. When you don't text, you're still sending a message. What I'm really showing here is that such behaviour is not tolerated and I can afford to cut her out and lose her. That's the deciding factor. Nonetheless, this was a tricky conversation to manage and as I work my way up the Texting Ladder she throws in a few more shit tests around the date request for good measure. God I love women. 😊

Remember, the stronger the test the more attracted they are.

So, there you have it gentlemen, shit tests. Whichever approach you adopt to deal with them, you need to ensure that you are not reacting to them. If you do, you'll have just handed over the frame to her and she'll lose respect for you. For the high-value women, one failed shit test will mean game over for you.

To the inexperienced, shit tests are scary and unpleasant, often dumbfounding a man as to what to do next to answer her test. However, with practice you can start to spot them and manage them as I have described. Once you start to become comfortable with shit tests you'll just view them as a small hurdle to overcome and a great indicator of her high interest levels.

5. Push-Pull

"Opposites attract…"

PUSH-PULL IS EXACTLY WHAT IT says on the tin. In the texting conversation you push her away, then you pull her in. It is flirting and brings colour and personality to your text messaging. Incorporating push-pull techniques into your texting is a must if you want to succeed in messaging women. If you follow the Texting Ladder too strictly, your messages will be straightforward and a bit boring. In addition, high-value women are usually in texting conversations with many men, so to stand out you're going to need to cause some trouble.

Let's first look at the push. As a minimum, the objective of the push is to spark a reaction. Similar to your school days in the playground, it's just like when a boy playfully pushes a girl away and she comes racing back to him with her response. The push shows you are confident enough to take risks with the relationship you have with her. The pull is when you are nice to her, giving her a compliment or a reward, thus pulling her in.

Just like Newton's Third Law, for every action there is an equal and opposite reaction. It doesn't matter whether you use a push or a pull first, just make sure that you use the opposite one next. Let's look at a simple example:

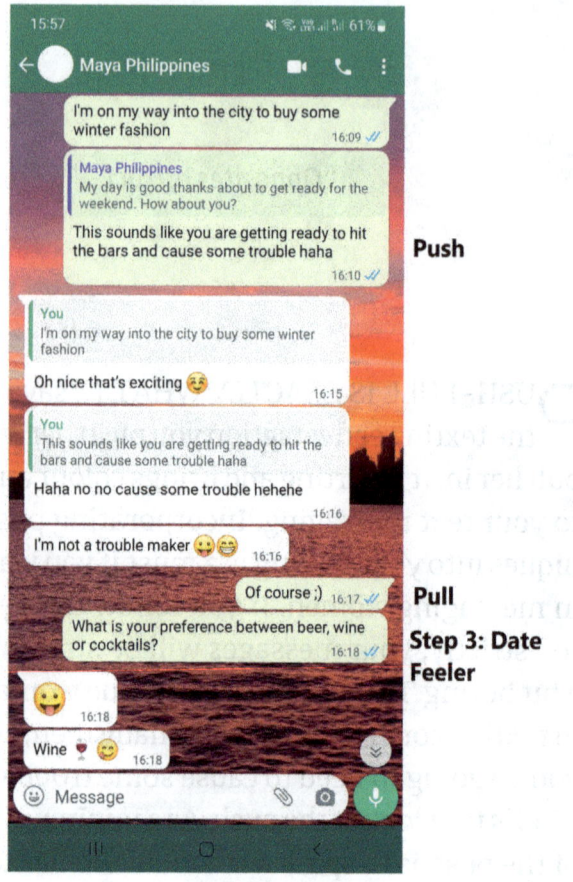

In this example, my light hearted push comes early on in the texting conversation. Her English speaking skills were average, so I tailor my push to be an easy to understand mischievous statement and add '*haha*' at the end to make sure she recognises my push. She reacts well, responding in kind and I give her a gentle pull, closing off the teasing and going for the date feeler.

So, when do you send push-pull messages? These take place on the middle of the Texting Ladder in normal conversation. They come after the opener and before the date request. They are a great filler for the build-up stage. Earlier in the book we talked about crescendos where the energy over text suddenly sparks into life like a fire, and that you can start to create crescendos when you get to more advanced levels of texting. Push-pull is one way to start those fires. Throw some petrol on the flames!

Here's an example of using push-pull to start and ride a crescendo all the way to a date request:

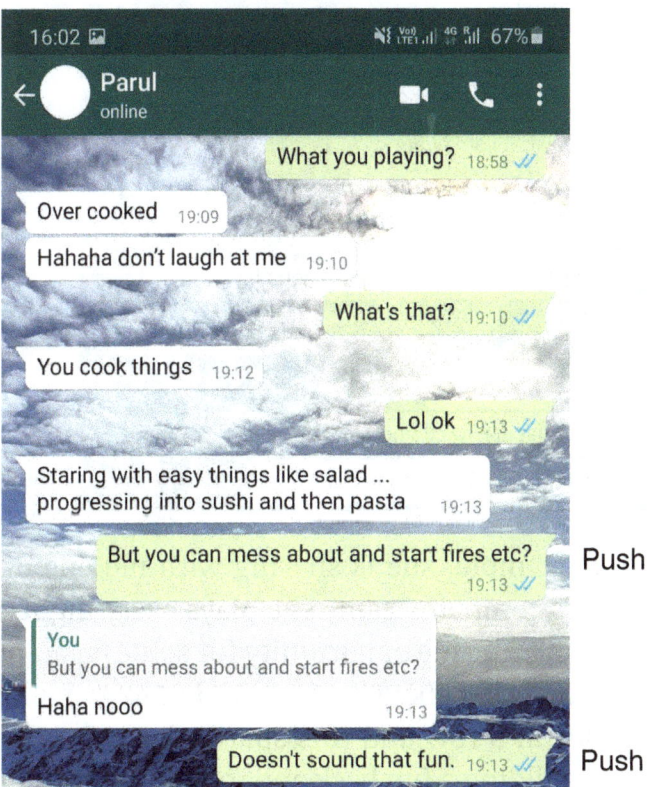

In this example, she is sharing with me one of her passions, a computer game she plays every night after work. Seeing a prime opportunity for some push-pull, I decide to tease her about her interest in this game. I push four times in a row and this sparks the conversation into life, building a fun back and forth conversation. At the end of the conversation she suggests I should play the game and I go for the pull, agreeing to the offer. This in turn generates a date request from her.

What you will notice here is I didn't rhythmically use push, then pull. I read the situation and used push or pull when it was appropriate to do so. In this case, I'm teasing a topic she is very invested in and it made it fun to keep pushing her about it. Like the example in the school playground I talked about earlier, sometimes the boy would playfully push the girl, who would push him back, thus starting a pushing match. Whilst it is fun, you can keep pushing each other over text message. However, be aware, if you push or pull too much in one direction, it will lose its fun because you are showing you are socially uncalibrated and not tuning into the conversation; like a child telling the same joke over and over again because they got a laugh the first time. You need to read the mood of the conversation carefully to watch when the push-pull vibes are starting to fade away and then move on, either towards a date request or back to normal conversation. If after having some push-pull and generating a crescendo you don't get to a natural date request or she refuses a date request, don't despair. You have still gained by showing you are prepared to take risks and have some fun. You will stand out compared to the other men she is texting.

So how do you know when to push and when to pull? That, my fine sirs, takes time and practice. Calibration is the key and we will talk more about that later. However, like everything in this book, give it a go and start practising.

6. Vacuuming

"Silence is golden."

VACUUMING IS A NICE AND easy technique to understand and apply. It basically means going quiet over the text message conversation and not writing anything for a few hours, days or even weeks. When you disappear like a phantom in the night, you create a void in the texting conversation. Your sudden disappearance means she is alone in the conversation, and if she's even slightly interested she'll wonder where you have gone and be sucked into the void you have created, filling it with her investment. This is vacuuming.

If everything is going well on the conversation and you are climbing up the Texting Ladder you don't need to vacuum. Vacuuming is used primarily to try to correct bad behaviours as a form of punishment, or to test her interest levels if you feel she is messing you around or playing games. In simple terms, high-value men do not tolerate being repeatedly messed around by women. Such men will play some games over push-pull and manage her tests, but any more trouble than this and a high-value man is simply not going to waste his time. They are busy, have other options with women, and vacuuming is a great way to either correct her behaviours or to eliminate her entirely from the contest of dating you. This is how you should think when it comes to texting women and employing the vacuum.

Vacuuming is also an excellent tool to utilise if you feel you have messed up the texting conversation. If you find yourself messaging too much and being needy or breaking the conversation through too much push-pull or telling a joke that didn't work, vacuuming should be your go-to technique. Vacuuming to correct your own mistakes is a great way to reset the conversation, reclaim the frame and start again.

The great thing about vacuuming is that you don't have to do anything! Simply don't text her: watch and wait. Let's look at an example:

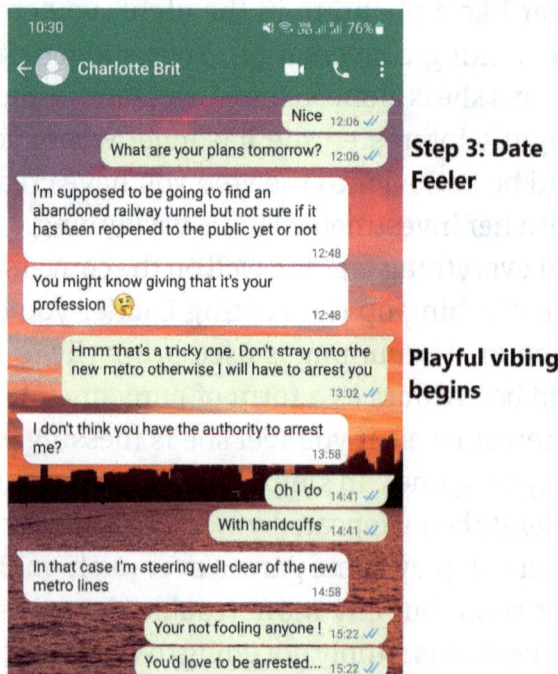

Vacuuming

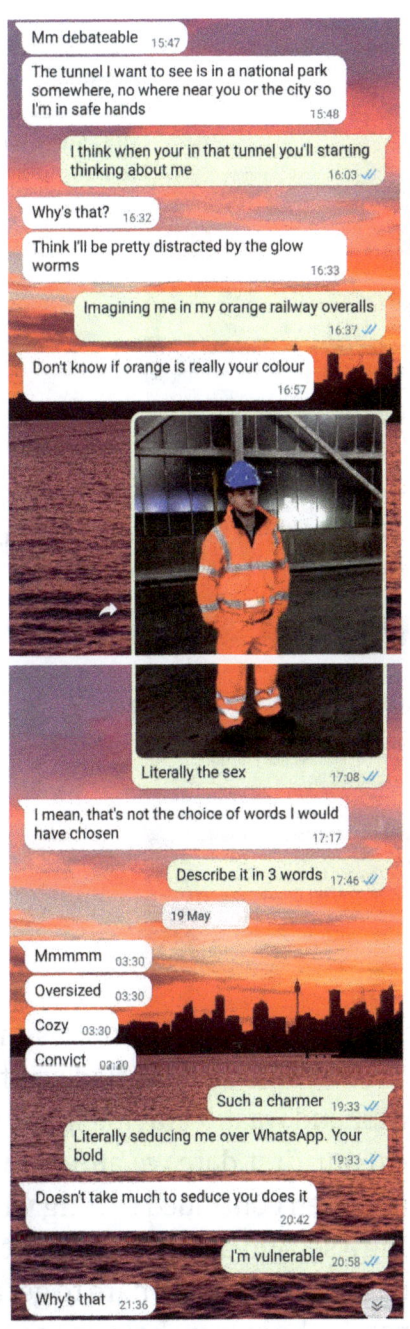

I engage in playful banter to see if I can climb back up the Texting Ladder and soften her game playing

More playful vibing

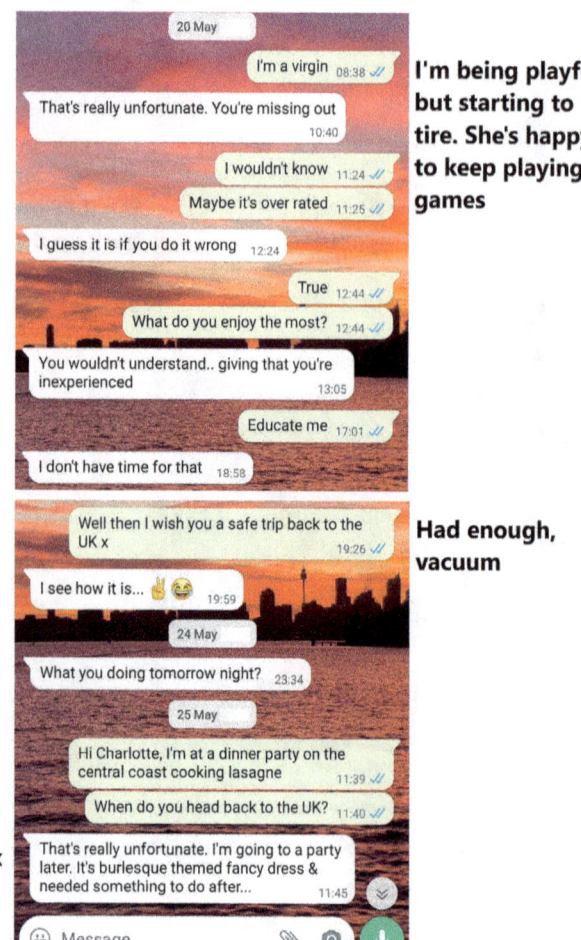

The background to this texting conversation is I met this girl on a street approach and then we had our first date. She was a backpacker and wasn't staying in my city for too much longer. On our first date we almost went back to my apartment and then continued texting where I had my eye on arranging a second date. Throughout the texting and the first date, she loved to play hard to get and exuded a lot of confidence. In the screenshots you can see me sending the date feeler for date number two, which she sidesteps. The texting conversation then turns into a frame battle which is conducted through playful messaging. However, after engaging in this for a while I feel it's going nowhere and sign off with my *"wish you a safe trip"* message showing I'm prepared to cut her off and never see her again and then vacuum. She now knows that I'm not prepared to play games and keep chasing her and thus, she gets zero attention from me here on in.

Four days later, she steps forward into the void I have created with her date feeler message. I answer back plainly and she then proposes a sex date. Her tough, playful frame is gone and she accelerates the texting conversation to Step 5: Date Logistics. To find out more on how to text girls who are playing games and vacuuming, you can watch my video here: 'How To Text A Girl Who Is Playing Hard To Get & Get Her To Ask You Out! Screenshot

Vacuuming directly supports frame control over text message. If she is willing to operate within your frame and generally behave herself then there are no issues.

However, if she starts playing games or messing you around she is directly challenging your frame, either in an attempt to seize it from you or to not comply with it., and you don't have frame if there's no one operating inside it. The setting for your frame in such scenarios is that you are a cool, high-value guy but you have your limits and won't be messed around. If she does mess you around she will get the silent treatment from vacuuming. This will either correct her behaviours and she will come back into your frame or she will identify herself as a time waster and you need to move on. Vacuuming is a great tool for filtering out women who are not interested in you which makes your text messaging far more efficient. I'm sure we all know guys who have been messaging a particular girl for years. The messaging stream is fun and flirty and there is a suggestive air of optimism about a possible meet up, but that date will never come, and she will always have an excuse. Don't waste your time on these women. Screen them by vacuuming and move on.

Now, what about the texting window of opportunity you told us about in chapter 2.6 I hear you cry! If I vacuum, won't this window close and all will be lost? There is some truth in this, however, you wouldn't vacuum if things were going well, and actually, to take a risk in this way and vacuum can buy you more time in the long run. If you vacuum and she doesn't step forward and fill the void, you have just filtered her out and you were climbing the Texting Ladder to nowhere. The texting window of opportunity was already closed on you, and you just found that out. However, if you vacuum and she is interested, she will fear your loss, step forward into the void and breathe life back into your texting conversation. The texting window of opportunity has been pushed open a bit more and you can resume your climb up the Texting Ladder to that date request.

Another very important reason you may want to use the vacuum is if you make a mistake in the text message conversation. It is a certainty that you will make mistakes and this can be anything from some push-pull that goes wrong, a date request sent too early, or just texting too much. This can lead you to losing the frame. Vacuuming is your best bet to recover the situation and put you back into the driving seat. Once you've recognised you've cocked things up, start the vacuum and go quiet for one to two weeks. If she texts you first before you've finished vacuuming then great! Recommence the texting conversation and start climbing back up the Texting Ladder. If she doesn't, wait until your one to two week time delay is up then ping her with a Step 2: Build-Up message. All should be forgotten by her after this vacuum and you can rekindle your conversation.

Applied correctly, vacuuming can be a very effective technique to turn around an otherwise troublesome conversation that is going nowhere. If the conversation does resume, you can often climb up the Texting Ladder quickly and head out onto a date. And if she doesn't reply, you just learned that she is not interested, and you didn't even have to send a single message to find that out.

7. Using Photos and Images

"A picture paints a thousand words."

USING PHOTOS AND IMAGES IS another very easy technique to pick up and should form a regular staple of all of your text message conversations with women. Any run of the mill texting conversation between two people will typically feature words: exchanging information. However, to add a new dimension to your texting conversation and make it a lot more interesting, you can send a photo or an image. So, what should you send? Sending a photo of something cool you are doing, or someplace noticeable is a great first move to learning this technique. There aren't really any limits to what you can send but it must be based on your frame which we have talked about throughout this book. This frame is that you are a high-value guy who is leading a busy, interesting life independent of women. The man about town. Operating from this frame means you would send a photo of a beautiful beach you are walking past, for example, or sending a photo of some local landmark you are visiting. However, if you are not doing anything particularly amazing don't let that hold you back. You can turn something average into something interesting.

More low-key photo messages that can still be effective could be a photo showing you are about to start playing your favourite sport or hobby, or you having a meal in your favourite restaurant or drinks in a bar with friends. The real message you want to be communicating with a woman when sending a photo is "I'm doing something interesting and I'm giving you an insight into my world." That's it. Let's look at an example:

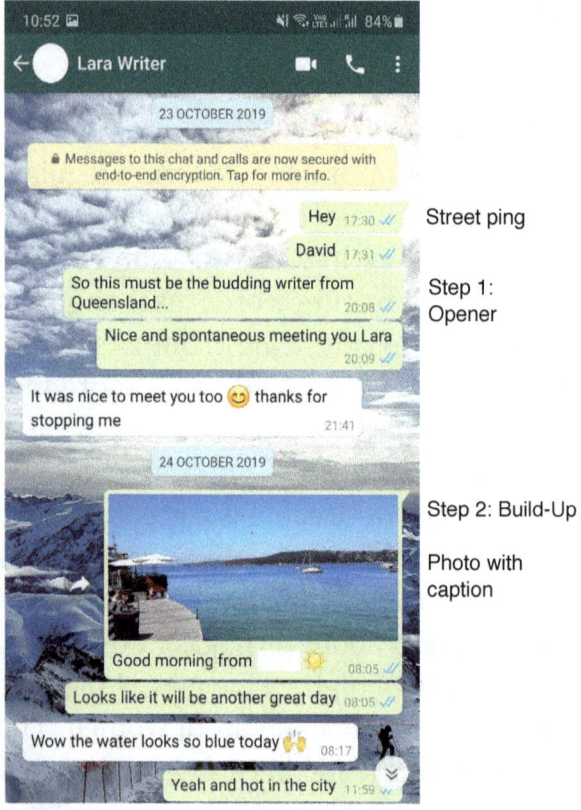

This is a basic photo message. Once she's replied to my opener I send a photo message of this pretty seaside view. I add a small caption and that's all I need to do. In terms of the Texting Ladder, photo messages are a good choice in the Step 2: Build-up stage to show you're an interesting guy and can make conversation as you progress towards the date request. Also, to recommence a texting conversation after a date or to reinvigorate a conversation that might have gone cold for a few days, kicking it off with a photo message can be a great way to start climbing back up the Texting Ladder. We call this the ping, or pinging. If you send photos or images, make sure you use them sparingly so that they add value to the conversation. Don't send them for every reply you make, it's too much investment from your side.

Once you have set a precedent for sending the occasional photo or image, you may find she starts to send you some of her own. This is a great sign of her investment levels in you. As we say at Team Thorpe, behaviour breeds behaviour. Here's an example:

In this example, the girl decides to send a revealing photo to qualify herself to my question. She is depicting that she is comfortable to show me her sexual side, operating inside my frame. If you receive these kind of photo messages from women your relationship with them is in a strong place. However, don't get too ahead of yourself. Whilst it is a great sign you are receiving these kind of messages, it doesn't mean you will seamlessly climb up the Texting Ladder, go on a date, and take her back to your house within 30 minutes. She may very well decide to test you, play a few games, and make sure you are also a worthwhile pursuit. Be careful with your reply; she will be watching you closely. If she sends a photo like the above example or something similar where she is looking hot, don't over compliment her in your reply. Most men would write back, "*Oh my god, wow, you look amazing!*" This puts her on a pedestal and you are handing over your frame. Don't do this. Instead, pay her a low-level compliment like "*nice*" or "*looking good.*" If you really want to drive a hard frame over text, you wouldn't even acknowledge the photo; you'd change topic and move the conversation onwards. Doing this will leave her not entirely satisfied and she will continue to chase you for validation. Not acknowledging a hot photo from her also gives the impression that you see these kinds of photos all the time and are comfortable around attractive women and are non-reactive.

You can also use photos or images in support of the other techniques we have explained in this book. One technique that is directly supported by using photos and images is push-pull.

In this scenario, you make an assumption or mischievous accusation about her and support it with a photo or image. You can easily do this by going on Google images, typing in your idea, like "bad party girl," find something suitable, download it, then send it. You can get quite creative and have fun at the same time! Here's an example:

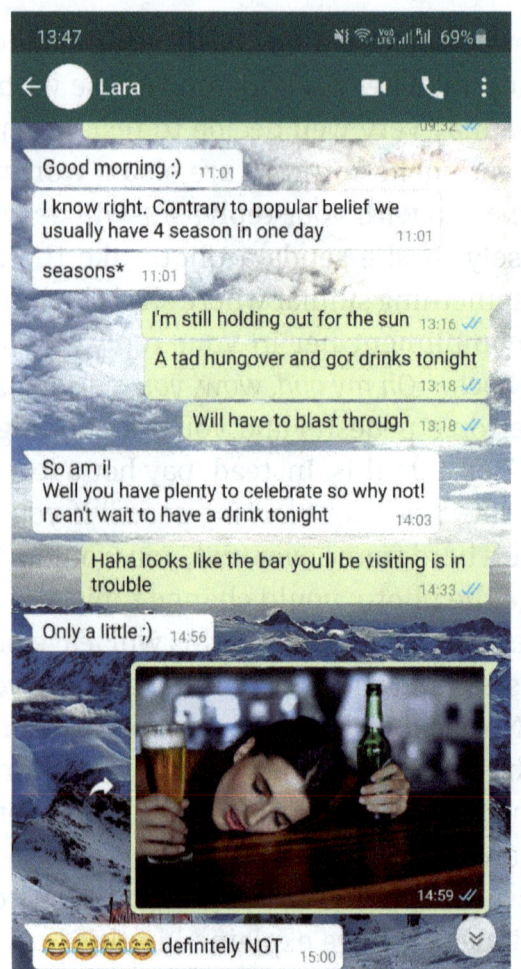

Push with a photo

Seeing an opportunity for a bit of mischief and a push, I go onto Google and look for a drunk girl image. Finding a suitable image, I send this. I don't need to provide a caption as it is pretty self-explanatory. This causes an amusing reaction on her side and the conversation advances on.

As you get to know a woman's personality better through dating, you can tailor your photo and image messages to the relationship you have with her. By doing this you will strengthen the bond you have which increases the likelihood that she'll continue to see you. In one such case, I gave the girl a nickname – "Kitty" – which she developed into a whole new persona! So, with this fun nickname established, it turned into a topic of conversation all by itself. Let's take a look:

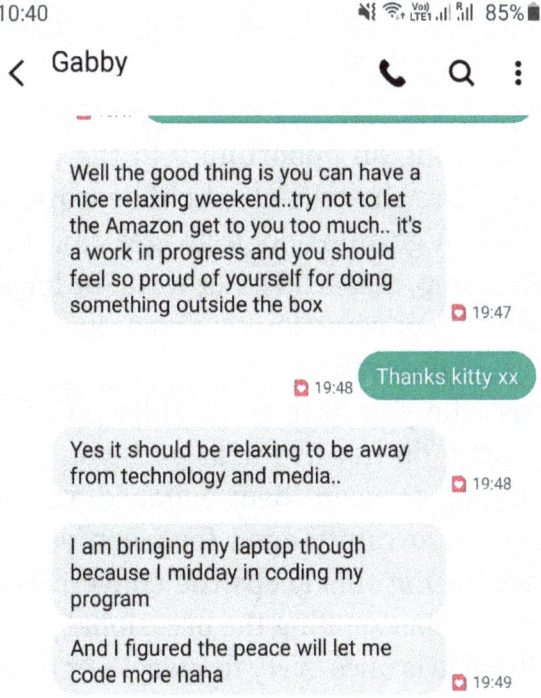

Tis me! But I look nerdier.. not such a cool cat

Again, spotting an opportunity in the texting conversation where she tells me she'll be working on her laptop, I simply go onto Google images, find an image of a cat on a laptop, and send it her way. She buys into the frame and our conversation continues in a fun manner for the rest of the evening.

For girls who you have an established relationship with and who do not live near you, you can employ photo pinging to keep them engaged and keep that window of opportunity open for when you return to their town. Doing this keeps the conversation interesting rather than sending the occasional greeting and asking how she is once every few weeks or months.

In one such instance, I collected the number of a girl in Serbia but ran out of time to see her on my visit. However, I kept the conversation going for over 2 years through occasional photo pinging and, when I returned to Serbia, we went out. Here is an example of a photo ping I used:

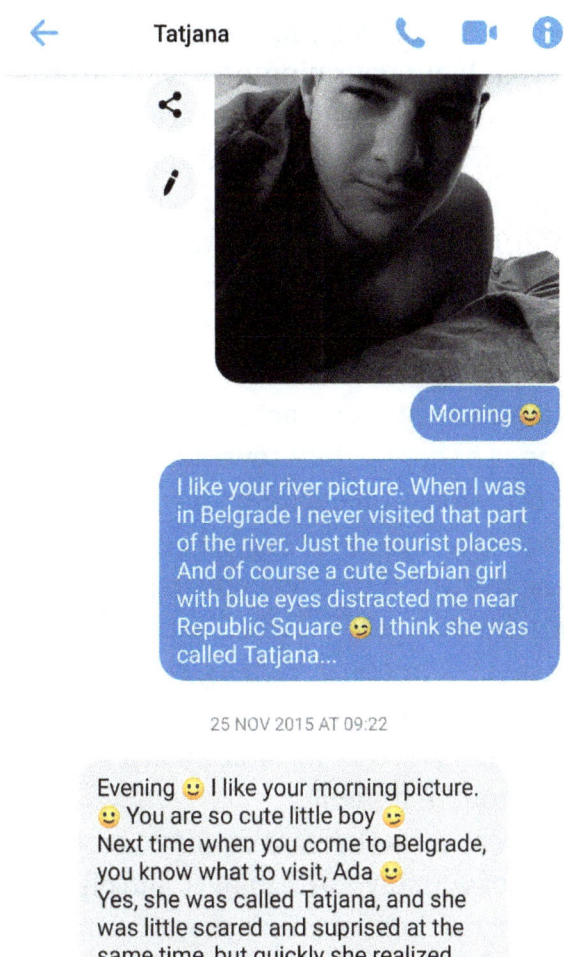

Here I send a photo of myself in bed in which I am looking surprisingly good in the morning! I then reminisce about my time in Belgrade and weave into the message my meeting her. Her reply is long, detailed, and complimentary which shows a good level of investment. In this scenario where you are overseas from the woman, photo pinging with a supporting message should be done once every few weeks or once a month. You can stretch out your pinging beyond this timeline, it just depends how connected you are with her.

In support of this long-term texting approach I never delete a number. I know many guys do when the conversation dries up, or they leave a place and move on. However, to do this means you have broken your communications link forever with her and you may find that from a photo ping you send a few months later, the conversation quickly picks up again as her circumstances have changed or her feelings towards you have changed. On some occasions, I have found a woman pinging me after a long time and as I've saved her number and not deleted the historical texting conversation I know who she is and where we got to on the Texting Ladder. On one such occasion I didn't hear from a girl for over 9 months. Then, one Saturday morning, she pinged me with, "*Want to be my friend?*" A few texts later I had a date booked in and we went out that night.

Another great tip we can pass onto you is that you can stockpile all of your favourite images and photos on your phone and reuse them as much as you want. It doesn't matter if the photo or image is a few years old. Use it! Often on a typical morning, I will resume all of my texting conversations with the same photo ping to kick off the day. Then progress each of the conversations up the Texting Ladder.

Sending photos and images to women demonstrates that you have a versatile communication skillset that you can harness over text messaging. Through the calibrated use of photos and images you can be flirtatious, interesting, charming, and mischievous.

8. The Holy Grail of Texting – the Audio Message

"Praise be, he spoke!"

SENDING AUDIO MESSAGES IS AN advanced technique which I urge you to start practising once you have mastered the other techniques in this book. Done correctly, audio messages can launch you up the Texting Ladder at breakneck speed. You can employ audio messages to support push-pull, circumnavigate her shit tests, build rapport, and use them to support your photo pings. Audio messages can also turn around difficult, troublesome conversations and unblock message streams that have hit a dead end. If you conquer the use of audio messages, there is no downside to them. Thus, they are the Holy Grail of texting. But, with great power comes great responsibility. You need to know what you are doing and you need to accept that if you get just one audio message wrong, your texting conversation can often be over. Before we explore this chapter further, let's look at a few ground rules for audio messages.

The first and most important rule is that you need to feel confident enough to do them. Audio messages are an escalation in texting which shows you can operate at the highest level of texting skill. Only really confident guys do them. If this isn't you, but you still want to try, good on you. There's only one way to learn and if you are prepared to take risks with your texting conversations, you are exactly the kind of guy who should be using audio messages.

The second rule is the suitability of your voice. The reason audio messages are so effective is because you are adding a totally new dimension to the texting conversation; sound. If you have a deep, masculine voice where you can speak assertively with solid pronunciation you will have women falling over themselves to date you. Your accent in your native language is also equally important to your sound. I am blessed with an English accent, which is largely popular wherever I travel. When I occasionally send audio messages in other languages, my English accent generally comes off quite well. However, you don't need to be English to do well: owning your native language and sound is the principal objective here. Women love different accents so if you are from a small, unknown country and can speak well in your chosen language your accent will be hard to place and thus intriguing. Remember, you don't need to sound like Barry White or enunciate like Jamie Foxx to be successful. Most guys' voices will do. You only need to worry if you sound like a strangled cat or a squirrel on helium. If you don't know what you sound like, record yourself on your phone and play the recording back to yourself. You will sound different to how you think you sound but as long as you are happy enough with your voice then you are good to go. If you genuinely don't know if you sound good, ask your friends or family so you know you will get honest feedback.

The third rule is to keep audio messages brief. The ideal duration is less than 1 minute. This is enough time to get your message across. If you speak for longer than this, i.e., several minutes, you are talking too much, qualifying, and you risk losing the frame. Most texting apps will also tell the receiver how long an audio message is, and if it's a long one she might not be even bothered to play it.

There are a few other items to mention. Don't employ audio messages for women who don't speak your language well, or at all. You might think sending an audio message in a language she doesn't understand is exotic or sexy, but most likely she'll get frustrated wanting to know what you said and you will have to spend the next few messages explaining yourself and back peddling. It's not a good look and the magic and mystery of an audio message will be lost. Coming back to the confidence rule, if she is online on the messaging app and you start to record an audio message, she will get an alert saying you are leaving an audio. If you then cancel the audio because you are not happy with it and start recording another, she will see you repeatedly recording audios but not receiving them, which is not a good look for you. And of course, if you are in this paralysis analysis of audio message recording you also risk accidentally sending one you are unhappy with from one false button press on your screen! To solve this problem, simply use the voice recorder app on your phone and record away until you get the right audio. Save it and send it to her.

Ok, so now that we have established some ground rules, let's look at a few examples. Except, how on earth will I share the content of my audio messages with you, dear reader? For the purposes of this marvellous book I will type them out.

Let's begin with a simple example. In this message stream I met this girl outside of a bar and took her number. I worked my way up the Texting Ladder but she refused my first date request so after a few days I was back to recommencing the conversation. To start the conversation in a different vain, I began with a short audio message:

> *"Good morning Michelle, hello, I'm enjoying a late morning on the beach before seeing accountants to help me establish my new business in preparation for later in the year. It's very sunny, very beautiful here. How are you? How is China?"*

My audio message is short at 23 seconds. I speak slowly and clearly. I'm saying nothing remarkable in the message other than I'm in a nice location by the beach and I'm demonstrating a bit of high value with reference to meeting accountants to set up a new business. I then ask her how she is. Her response is positive and the texting conversation is kicked off with fast replies. Notice my follow-up messages are brief and I'm asking no questions. We have a good build-up phase over normal messaging and then I sign off, recognising that she will take her flight shortly. This is a good foundation to move towards the date feeler and date request when she's back in my town. Keeping your audio message simple and saying nothing extraordinary is a smart way to ease yourself into this technique and to learn the effectiveness of using your voice in a message.

Once you get comfortable sending basic audio messages you can bring in the other techniques you have learned in this book. In the next example, I brand the girl as a man-eater and give her a flirty push over audio to spike the conversation up.

The background here is that I have already been on one date with this girl. In my audio I say:

> "Good evening Lara, and yes, I can imagine that you have been terrorising my country's fair men in the city, mercilessly I'm sure. It's nice to hear from you, you have been in my thoughts as well. Likewise, I have just got back home. We are having a rainy storm here, quite cold, and I am also on my sofa with

my Arabic cushion, having a lager and listening to some old school Linkin Park. Absolutely rocking my Saturday."

I speak slowly and clearly, taking my time. Notice my audio message is less than one minute. The response from her couldn't be more positive. As we have said throughout the book, if you can get a reaction from her, this is a good thing. In terms of the Texting Ladder, I have had one date with this girl and we are back to normal conversation in the build-up stage. I'm still a while away from a second date request, so to spice up the conversation I use an audio message. It was positive for her and she refers to my accent a second time, further down the message stream. Not only has this audio message been effective, she has also told me she likes them. Therefore, for this conversation I know to use them again.

To be calibrated with audio messages means you don't want to use them all the time. However, randomly deploying them into your conversation is a great tactic. Don't be disheartened if she doesn't send her own audio message reply; women also need to have high levels of confidence to send their own back to you. However, if she is confident you may find her joining you on the audio precedent you have set. This shows strong investment on her part where she is mirroring you. With this in mind, audio messages can also be a great way to start those crescendos we talked about earlier in the book. To send an audio message escalates the conversation and it can be just the kickstart you need to encourage a flurry of text messaging that helps you to race up the Texting Ladder to the date request.

Now let's look at where an audio message can get you out of a difficult spot and make a big difference. In this example, I'll be referencing a conversation with a really hot, very personable Brazilian girl. I met her on a street approach and it was clear she was a high value women with plenty of confidence. Working my way up the Texting Ladder for the first date wasn't easy. She was sending plenty of tests but I managed to book her in for the first date. Then, the day before the date, she sends this:

In her long monologue you can see her arguing with herself before cancelling. There are a few observational points I take before deciding on my response. The first is she is writing a lot, which means she is very invested. Regardless of the cancellation, there is a lot of energy from her side. The second is her cancellation is emotional, not logical. She's not cancelling on me because her boss asked her to work late, she's cancelling on me because she can't reconcile the fact that we'll be meeting face to face.

She is in two minds and fighting herself, leading to indecisiveness which ultimately falls onto a cancellation. On the one hand she's very attracted to me which I deduce from the texting up until this point, but on the other hand she feels she doesn't have enough of a connection with me and that she's stereotyped me too much as a bad boy. She has got herself quite worked up and put herself under a lot of pressure because she knows that if she goes on a date with me something will probably happen between us.

Employing the usual, written text message techniques simply won't cut it for this type of emotional blockage.

The key that unlocks this conversation is the audio message. Understanding her resistance, I use an audio message that eases the pressure by acknowledging we don't know each other that well, but that I like her and want to go for a drink. Keeping it simple, my objective is to allay her fears. In the audio, I want to show her that I am a normal guy who is relaxed and easy going. I'm trying to generate a bridge between us that she can hopefully cross. It's the normality I convey and the sensitivity to her feelings that win the day here. Only an audio message can deliver this. An audio message gives her another whole dimension from which to relate to me, providing a much higher level of communication where she can deduce intent and make judgements from my tone, articulation, and sound. She may even be reminded by our first face-to-face meeting which further builds a connection. At Team Thorpe we generally advise against being the nice guy, but on this occasion bringing a softer, more understanding approach worked and we have the audio message to thank for that.

You can watch a full breakdown of this conversation and listen to the audio message on my YouTube channel, video titled 'She Cancelled Our Date - How To Reply Over Text & Get The Date Back'

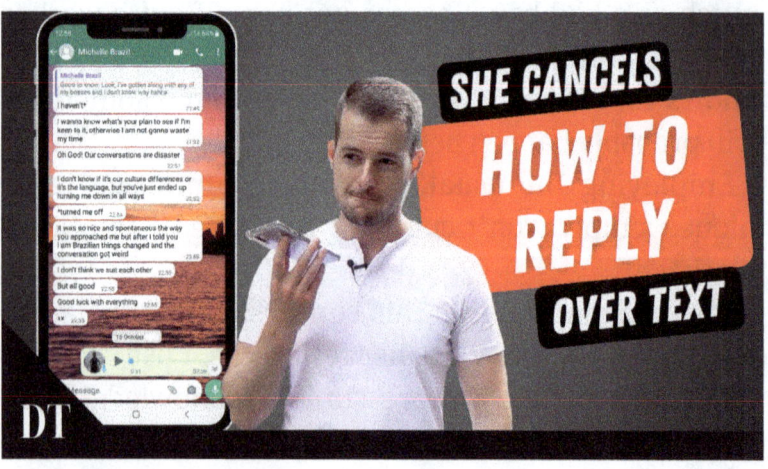

Audio messages can be high risk, so if you are climbing up the Texting Ladder without any real issues you don't need them. Follow the proven route and stick to text. Generally, I wouldn't recommend using audio messages on your first climb up the Texting Ladder. However, if you fall at the last step on the Texting Ladder and go back to Step 2, that would be the appropriate time to send an audio message and to try something different. The audio message could make the difference in your second climb up the Texting Ladder to securing that date. If you have been on one date or have an established relationship with her, the use of audio is a great way to keep your conversation alive and interesting.

There really is no limit as to what you can say over an audio message. Similar to a photo or an image ping, they give her an insight into your world, providing the stimulus of sound that sparks her interest and makes a world of difference.

9. After the first date: When and what to text

"I had a really great night..."

AFTER THE LAUNCH OF THE first edition of this book, this was the most requested chapter from guys for the second edition. So, here it is!

Ok, so you've successfully climbed the Texting Ladder, booked her in and went on that date. Congratulations!

Assuming you like her and want to continue seeing her, you'll need the medium of texting to secure date number two.

Again, we'll be using the Texting Ladder as our structure but with some subtle variations. So, when do you text her? I typically leave it around 24 - 36 hours after the first date before sending my first message. For example, if I went on a date with a girl on Monday evening, I'd text her Tuesday evening or Wednesday morning.

There are a few reasons as to why I leave it this amount of time. The first is, I don't want to appear too keen and to maintain an element of mystery and suspense. Going quiet for a day leaves the girl wondering if she will hear from me, which gets her thinking about me and builds some tension. In this case, a little absence makes the heart grow fonder. If you went crashing into her messages the following morning, there is no mystery and thus you are the chaser and she is the chased. The frame is moving over to her.

Second, leaving it this amount of time gives her the opportunity to come forward and text me first. This is not only a great ego boost for you, but it also communicates her interest levels and signals she couldn't deal with the tension and had to message first. Now she is the chaser, and you are the chased. Nice!

Allowing this short gap in texting maintains, and can even increase attraction from her side and sets you apart from needy guys who are in constant chase mode.

Let's look at an example:

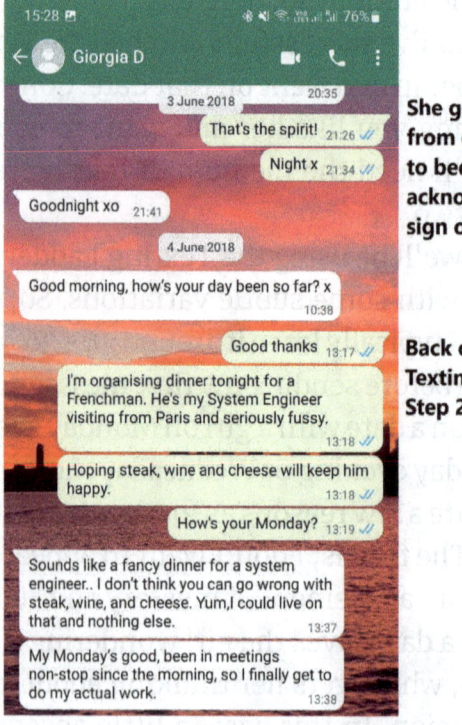

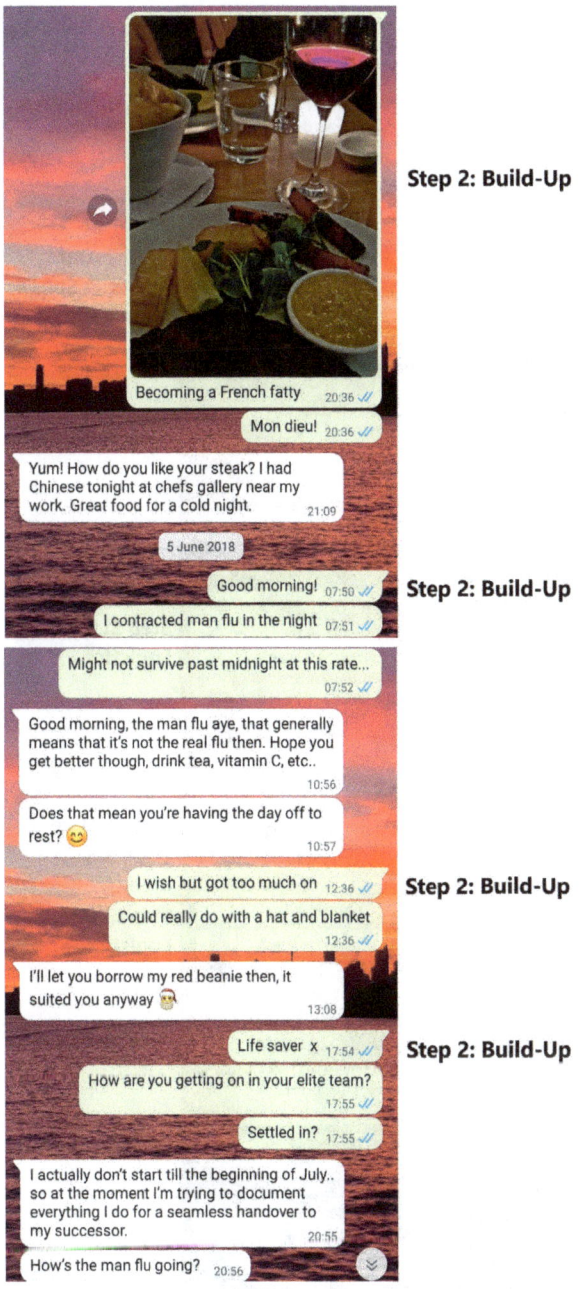

With this conversation, I was planning on leaving the texting conversation alone for a full 24 hours after our first date before messaging. However, she steps forward and messages me the following morning. I don't need to stick to my 24 hour rule now and respond after a few hours with my Step 2: Build-Up which would have been the same if I was messaging her first.

To make this second climb up the Texting Ladder a little different, I send a photo of my restaurant dinner, having not sent any images on the first climb up the Ladder. I then hold at Step 2: Build-Up stage for seven messages. I'm going with the flow here and don't want to ask her out straight away. Once this Step 2: Build-Up conversation starts to tail off, I send her a combined Step 3: Date Feeler and Step 4: Date Request. Tailoring the conversation to the girl, I know she loves bars and drinks and has been to most of the bars in Sydney City, so I don't need to build up some anticipation through a Date Feeler for a bar she has probably already been to. Plus, we have a solid connection from our first date so I just ask her straight out. I could have rigidly stuck to the Texting Ladder and sent a Step 3: Date Feeler, but it doesn't really matter in this situation. I make a judgement on the girl, her interest levels and our texting conversation and jump up the Texting Ladder in two steps.

With her accepting, we arrange Step 5: Date Logistics. Now, you'll notice at my message, *"Ok let's do town hall for 6pm,"* that she doesn't confirm this. I'm pretty confident the date is on, but just to make sure I send a confirmatory, *"All good for later"* to which she confirms and the date is booked in.

Another point to make is if you are on holiday and dating the local talent, leaving a 24 – 36 hour gap between your first date and texting might be too long, especially if you are coming to the end of your holiday. If this is you, just start messaging her earlier and see if you can get her booked in for date number two asap. You don't have anything to lose if you are leaving town shortly.

In short, how do you go about texting to secure date number two? Use the Texting Ladder but make sure you send slightly different content than you did the first time you climbed up the Ladder. If you sent an image of your cat on the first climb up the Ladder, send an image of a local landmark or cool restaurant as part of your Step 2: Build-Up. You don't need to do anything extraordinary on your second, third, or fourth climb up the Ladder. Just keep things simple and organic and follow the structure.

If you find on this second climb up the Ladder her responses have become smaller, slowed or stopped then she might have lost interest after your first date. For when she's not replying to you, head to Chapter 17.1.

10. How not to text

"Please love me! I'll do anything!"

EVERY ONCE IN A WHILE, we need to see someone perform really bad at something to appreciate that we're not doing too badly ourselves. And, if you see yourself in this poor performer, then it's great to admit you're at square one because the only way is up!

In this chapter I'll show what not to do when texting a girl. From this example, you should hopefully see everything you learned so far from this book has resonance and utility and in particular, the value in the last chapter we covered on securing that second date.

These screenshots came from a rare female fan at the time of the first edition of this book, who was keen to share one particular conversation of texting a guy she had experienced one date with. Whilst the first date didn't go that well, his texting afterwards confirmed they won't be going on a second date. Let's take a look:

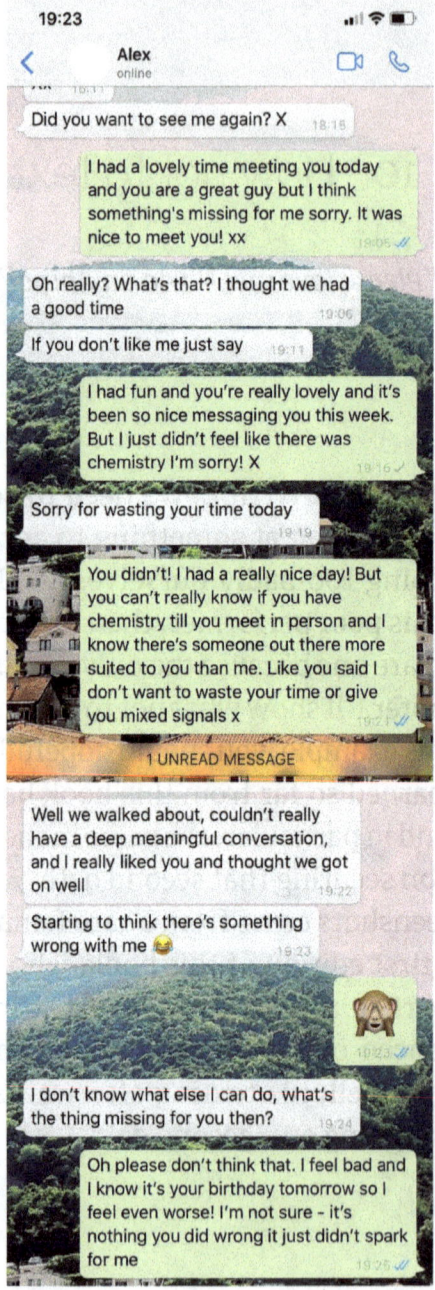

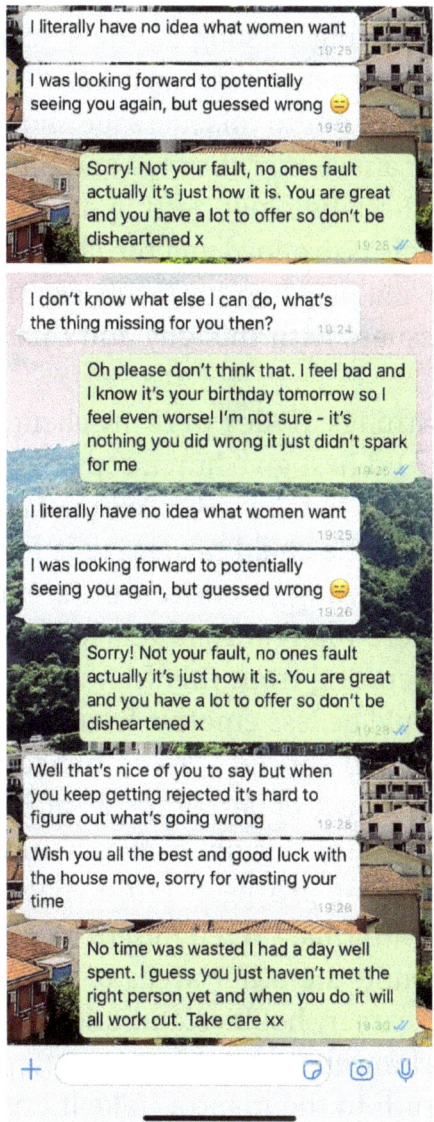

Jees! Where do we begin?! For me, this interaction reeks of neediness. This guy is operating from a position of no frame, no abundance and displays plenty of 'playing the victim' vibes. And worst of all, he's happy to play out these terrible traits over text message with girls. It goes wrong as soon as the screenshots start with the "*Did you want to see me again?*" I'm told there was no build up prior to this message and so this needy date request came out of the blue and hit the girl cold. When he realises he's not getting a second date, the dating dynamic is dropped and the chat nosedives into desperation and pleading for feedback. There's a certain hopelessness with this guy and I have some pity for him.

Now, to learnings. If Alex were my client, what would I say to him? I'd first give him a copy of this book and tell him he needs to follow the Texting Ladder. But the biggest learning he could take away is learning about frame and presenting an entirely different frame over text; one where his reality is relaxed, confident and assertive. Operating from this frame would mean his messages would be less emotive from a negative position, simpler and shorter. That's not to say he isn't allowed to feel needy or desperate, we all have and do at moments, but the skill is not to communicate this outwardly with dating prospects but manage it inwardly. And to help with this, I'd tell him to take a break from dating and build the other areas of his life a bit; his friendships, career, hobbies and take a short holiday to rebalance himself.

There is truth in the mantra 'fake it until you make it,' not to the point that Alex is a completely different person over text, but enough to radically change his communication style so he gets better responses from women.

Back in 2013, texting as a confident, assertive guy was strange for me because it wasn't really who I was when it came to communicating with women. But I was determined to learn, practice, and make the necessary changes to my texting skills and actually found out over time I was quite the mischievous texter! Assimilating the texting skills in this book with your personality is something we will cover in the last chapter.

What key takeaways can you see in the screenshots? What would you say to Alex to help him?

11. Managing Psycho Girls Over Text

"I love you! I hate you!"

THERE ARE NUTTERS IN EVERY society and a gentleman is sure to come across a few psycho girls in his dating life. And, like taking that attractive Thai girl home in Bangkok, only to find "Kanlaya" is actually called "Kevin," sometimes it won't be immediately obvious who you are dealing with until it's too late. In this chapter I'll show you when to recognise you're dealing with a problem girl and what to do about it.

A while ago, I was on my way home from work and spotted a cute South American girl walking the opposite way. Seizing the opportunity, I ran back, approached and after a few minutes suggested an instant date. Little did I realise I'd just strayed into a mine field...

We head to the local bar and one drink in, she bursts into tears and is inconsolable. No gents, it wasn't my killer chat about Blackburn Rovers being the greatest football team on earth; this girl had a lot of problems. Over a teary Chardonnay, all her issues came flooding out. It emerged she had endured a terrible childhood and had been single most of her adult life. Now aged 32, she was feeling the pressure to settle down and there wasn't a budding suitor within a thousand miles.

At rare moments like this, I drop the whole dating dynamic and listen as best I can. After the drink, I gave her my number and made clear she can contact me if she wants help with her corporate job (another problem of hers) but dating isn't on the agenda going forward.

However, for her, I might as well have said let's get married next week and have 10 children.

That evening she starts blowing up my phone and texts me multiple times per day. A week later, I go to England for a holiday and she demands that I invite her and then throws tantrums when she gets no reply. When I return, her texting tirade continues. Take a look:

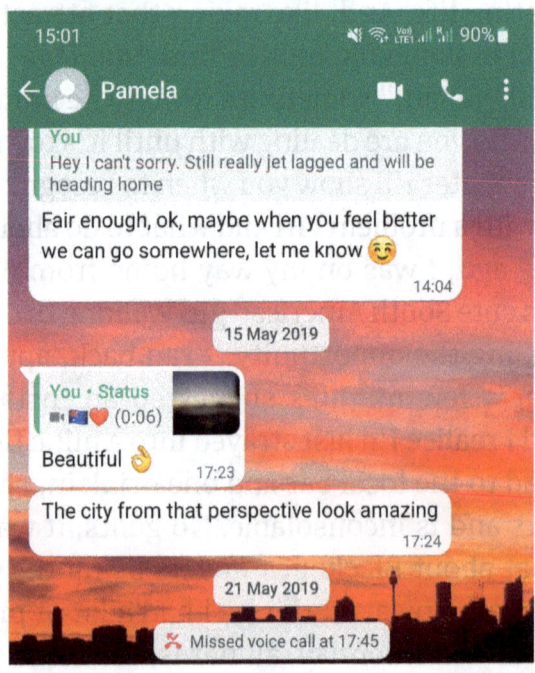

This is only a fraction of what she was sending over that period. From the screenshot you can see she is the only one texting and chasing, asking me out and calling me. When she starts imagining that I'm walking around the streets in sports clothes I block her.

WhatsApp, Telegram and Signal gave us a fantastic tool to deal with such girls and that is to block them. And if she's proper mental, you might want to go into your contacts app and see if you can block her there as well for good measure so she doesn't start sending SMS's or try calling you.

These types of girls may threaten you, give you ultimatums etc, but all you need to do is not react and block them.

I wanted to include this chapter in the book to warn the more inexperienced guys reading this. When you start out on improving your dating life, any interest shown by women is welcomed where previously you had little or none. This was me back in 2013. However, what you can see here is a different type of attention.

It's desperation and delusion, not attraction. Whether it's their fault or not, some girls are damaged goods and you would do well to steer clear of them. Don't delude yourself in thinking she must be very interested and book in a date. Dating and taking such a girl home could put you in a seriously dangerous position. I don't care if you haven't had a date in a while! Stay at home, put your feet up and watch the football 😊.

Luckily for me, this girl identified herself early on and was thus easy to eliminate from the contest of dating me.

12. Broadcast Lists

"This is Operator Thorpe, calling all units..."

THIS CHAPTER IS FOR GUYS who have lots of numbers in their phone and are time constrained. Whether you're a pro street approacher or internet dating master, congratulations on having lots of numbers and options with women.

WhatsApp, Signal and Telegram all have the broadcast feature when it comes to sending messages. Broadcast lists are a one-to-many messaging tool. Specifically referring to WhatsApp broadcast lists from here on in, you can send a message to several of your contacts at once. A broadcast list is a saved list of contacts that you can send broadcast messages to without having to select them each time. This removes the need to copy and paste the same message. This is not the same as a WhatsApp group, where everyone can see what everyone else is posting in a forum. Whilst you see the same message go to all the girls in your broadcast list, for the girl, she just sees a message from you. If she replies, the reply goes back to just you, not your whole broadcast list.

If you are collecting a lot of numbers in a short space of time and finding it difficult to keep up with all the texting, bundling all the girls you have on your radar into the broadcast list can be useful. I've found broadcast lists particularly beneficial when I'm overseas on holiday in party environments and collecting many numbers. In this scenario, I use a broadcast list to send the same Step 2: Build-Up message to many girls. This message is a standard ping to see which girls are out there and interested.

For example, I'd send an image of myself on the beach or a photo of a local landmark I saw that day, write some accompanying text like, *"Loving the beach in Copacabana today"* then maybe a *"how are you?"* and send this. The great thing about doing this is, its minimal effort for you to send the message and then all you need to do is sit back and wait for any interested girls to reply. For the girls that do respond, simply continue the conversation in each individual chat and resume the tailored messaging and don't forget to use her name every now and then. I wouldn't continue to use broadcast lists beyond this initial Step 2: Build-Up message. The broadcast list has done its job in telling you which girls are interested and therefore which ones you should focus on to securing a date. It's similar to a mass screening exercise.

Now yes, I know I said in chapter 2.1 Say My Name Say My Name that you should address the girl by her name in most of your messages, but sending just one Step 2: Build-Up message through a broadcast list every now and then shouldn't limit your chances.

Here's how you set up a broadcast list on WhatsApp:

1. Go to WhatsApp and select the more options, represented by 3 vertical dots. Select new broadcast.
2. Search for or select the contacts you want to add to the broadcast list.
3. Tap the check/tick mark to add the contacts to the broadcast list.
4. Inside the blank broadcast list chat, select the more options button, represented by 3 vertical dots and select Broadcast list info. Here you can change the name of the list to something like, Girl Leads Broadcast. In this menu you can also add more contacts to the broadcast list.
5. Go back to the broadcast list chat and send your first message. Sit back and watch the replies roll in!

Now one thing to note is if you can't find a particular girl you want to add to your broadcast list, and you know she is a contact of yours, this is because she has not added you to her contact's book. In this case you can't add her so leave her out of your broadcast list.

So there you have it gents, another useful tool for your texting toolbox. Generally, when I'm in my home city, I don't use Broadcast lists. I don't have tons and tons of girls to text per week and therefore can focus on a tailored conversation for each girl. However, when I'm overseas partying away and not taking texting too seriously, broadcast lists have been a real time saver.

13. Phone Calls

"Call me David..."

PHONE CALLS IN A TEXTING book? Really? Damn right! Phone calls are one of the most powerful techniques in the book and even rival the audio message in Chapter 8. In one brief phone call you can cover off all five steps of the Texting Ladder, book her in for a date and stand out from the other guys she's in contact with.

However, like audio messages, phone calls require high levels of confidence and are fraught with risks. Used incorrectly, they can scare off women and kill your relationship with her in an instant. Alas, fear not dear reader for I shall show you how to boss phone calls!

So, why would we call women in this day and age? Whilst it's old school, it's refreshing and far more effective in communicating emotions and intent. Many women will appreciate a call and sit up and take notice of you during the dating journey. Plus, you'll be only one of a few guys who are doing this. In addition, if you are a super busy, successful guy you may not have the time in your day to work through the Texting Ladder and so calling her can be a great alternative. Calling her in between your appointments on a short break may very well suit your routine and communication style. And, with a brief structure I'll provide you for your phone call, you can leapfrog days of texting and book her in for a date there and then.

When in the dating journey would we call a women we're interested in? Typically, after date number two or date number three. This ensures some familiarity and connection between the two of you and increases the chance she will pick up the phone and engage in the conversation. If I do decide to do a phone call, I'll call her midweek, one evening after work around 8pm or 9pm. This time increases the likelihood she'll pick up and calling in the middle of the week gives me a good amount of runway to book in a weekend date.

Before we explore this chapter further, let's look at a few ground rules for calling women.

The first and most important rule is that you should never leave a voicemail if she doesn't answer. You are suddenly put on the spot by her telecom company to leave a snappy message with no chance of correcting it if you bugger it up. As soon as you hear that bleep, hang up! If you want to hear how bad (and funny!) voicemails can be for guys and girls dating one another, check out BBC's flirt divert videos on YouTube.

Following on from this, the second rule is if she doesn't pick up, do not call her again. And don't leave a follow up text either, like, *"hey, I just tried calling you."* She will have a notification on her phone saying you called and having no voicemail or text message from you will add some intrigue and mystery for her and increase the chance she will call you back.

The third rule is if she does answer, keep the conversation to around 5 minutes in length. You do not want to be blabbing on and on over the phone like she's your best friend. Keep it short.

Ok, so for a conversational structure for a phone call I use this:

1. Hello's
2. Ask her how she is
3. Ask a specific question about something going on in her life; how is her work, assignment, prep for sports event etc
4. Listen to her answer on point 3 and ask follow up questions on this topic. This is called ploughing or tunnelling. Stay on topic!
5. She might ask you a question or two. Answer these
6. Date Feeler
7. Date Request
8. Finish call, hang up

With this structure, you are still following the Texting Ladder, just over a phone call. Points 2 to 5 are the Build-Up. Points 6 and 7 are the Date Feeler and Date Request. If she answers positively to points 6 and 7, I say something like, "*great, I'll send you the meeting time and location over text later*" and then finish the call. This is the Step 5: Date Logistics step and I don't do this over the phone simply because most women won't remember the specifics of the date location and time. I also do this to not appear too keen and to show I'm a relaxed guy who doesn't need 100% confirmation to my date there and then.

The following day after the call, I'll send one of these texts, covering Step 5: Date Logistics.

> **Copy & Paste Zone**
>
> Hey, good to chat last night. For Thursday, meet me at 6pm in the main square by the tree.
>
> Hey, good to talk the other day. For the weekend, lets meet on Sunday, 1pm by the train station entrance.

All you need is for her to reply and confirm this and you have your date booked in. And thus, in one short phone call and one text message you've climbed the Texting Ladder. Nice work!

Now, if she's very keen on the call and asks you where specifically to meet and at what time, provide this information. Then, a day or two later I'd still send one of the above text messages to confirm.

Another point to mention is I only do phone calls with girls who I know are confident and outgoing. It takes courage for the girl to pick up the phone too, so if she's shy or English isn't her first language, just stick to texting.

I understand you may not be interested at all in phone calls and want to stay well clear of this technique. That's fine and you don't need to do them. Most of my conversations with women in between dates are purely text and audio messages.

However, I do urge you to try them out and build this skillset. Over the years, I have found phone calls particularly useful for girls who aren't keen on texting. What I perceive to be a lead fading away is suddenly abolished when she quickly picks up the phone and engages enthusiastically in a phone call and happily agrees to a date. I've also found phone calls to be very beneficial for the very hot, high value, in demand girls who are busy and constantly being chased by guys over text. Giving them a call (and it going well!) really makes you stand out and can make the difference in securing that date. Phone calls are not a part of my regular toolbox of booking in women for dates, but as and when you need to, call her.

14. Nao Entendo – Girls Who Don't Speak Your Language

"Parlez-vous Anglais?"

EVERY NOW AND THEN YOU'LL come across a girl who doesn't speak your language. Many guys simply write these women off as dead ends and move on. However, I'll show how you can communicate with these women and book them in for dates.

The answer is to use the Google Translate app with some of my additional words of advice.

Simply download Google Translate on your phone and select the language you are writing in and the language you want to translate to. Once you've typed what you want, hit enter and boom, there is your message in her language. You even have a copy icon to save the text before moving into your messaging app and pasting it there. One cool option is in the settings you can download an entire language's vocabulary locally to your phone. This is useful if you are travelling and don't want to burn data on the move or Wi-Fi isn't readily available.

Things to bear in mind when texting women over Google Translate is the translation will never be perfect and on occasion, parts of the message will be lost in translation. Google Translate will perform the literal translation for you but won't provide the interpretation, local expressions or colloquialisms. As a result, you'll be working at a slight disadvantage but you can counter this by keeping your texting really simple. No need to be mischievous with some Push Pull or charming with an Audio message. Stick to the Texting Ladder plainly in your language to give Google Translate the best chance of converting your message across and get her booked in for that date. Let's take a look at an example from my time in Brazil. Apologies for the mushiness of this message stream, Yasmin was one of my Rio Carnival romances. If you go to Rio Carnival, you'll understand 😉:

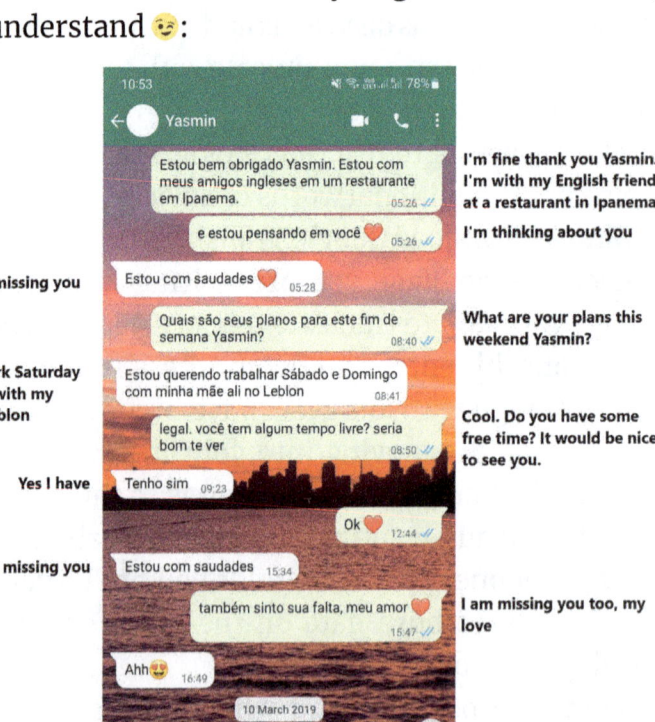

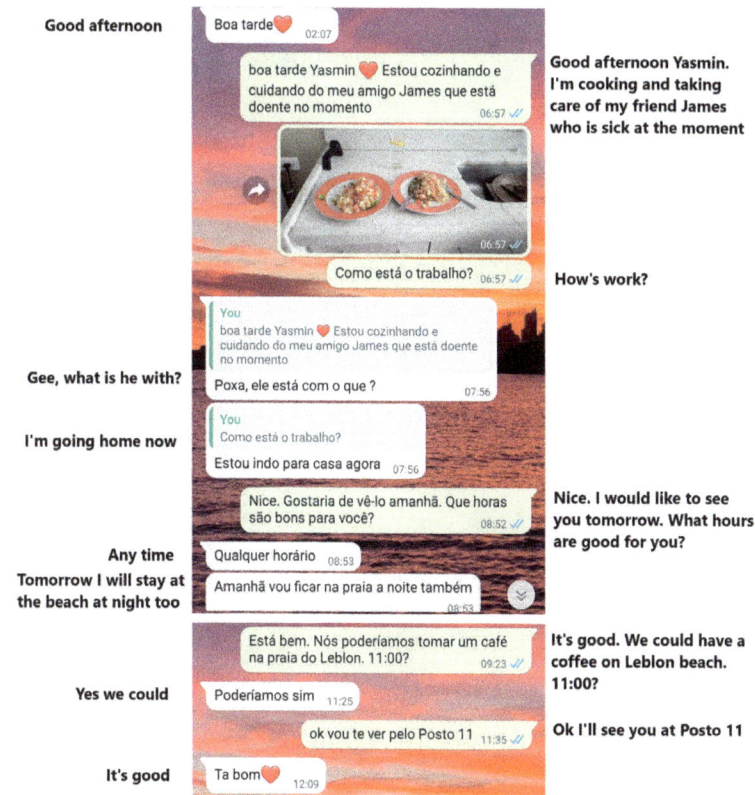

For this entire messaging stream, I'm using Google Translate from English to Portuguese and copying and pasting the messages over into WhatsApp. You can see my Step 2: Build-Up messages I send are simple, plain and easy to understand. My messaging then transitions to booking her in for a date over Steps 3, 4 and 5 of the Texting Ladder. That's it. There's no point trying to be clever over text, just focus on getting that date arranged. Whilst it is a hassle to switch between Google Translate and your messaging app, the alternative is to either not text these foreign beauties or learn the language yourself. Clearly then, Google Translate is a useful tool for the travelling man.

15. How to break up over text

"It's not you, it's me..."

IN THIS CHAPTER I'LL SHOW you how to break up a short term relationship over text message. But let's tackle the elephant in the room. Why would you put the effort into telling her you don't want to see her anymore? Why not do the bloke thing and just not text her until she gets the hint?

These are, indeed, relevant questions gentlemen. So, let's face them head on.

The main reason we should do this is because we are respectful, confident, honest men. We don't fear taking hard decisions and we move assertively. Whilst this is essential when we are pursuing women, it's equally essential when we don't want to see a woman anymore. By telling her directly, we're not wasting her time and not wasting our time anymore. There's no need to run and hide whenever she texts you, kicking the can down the road to deal with her next time as she wonders why you're ghosting her. Also, older women are on a more pressing schedule than we are as they look to fulfill their biological agenda of settling down and having children. Furthermore, I feel we all have a duty as men to build credibility amongst our sex where previously, masculinity has taken a significant beating by society and still does today. While she might not like the message you are delivering, she won't be able to argue with the honesty of it and ultimately respect you for being upfront and give a plus point to masculinity generally. By doing this, you are also helping out the next guy who comes along and dates her. If we all did this, I think we'd find women wouldn't become so disillusioned and disengaged with dating men.

Another key reason we do this is because it strangely leaves the door open to reengage with the girl and start dating them again. Whilst this doesn't work all the time, I have done this countless times in my formative years when I couldn't make my mind up with casual relationships and more long term relationships. Because I did tell women that I didn't want to see them anymore, most of them would hold some admiration and respect for me and thus re-engage when I did. Flip flopping between relationships with women is not a modus operandi I would recommend and having my time again I would have done things differently, but it was remarkable how I could restart relationships after previously telling a girl it was over. However, if I'd been a pussy and ghosted her until she got the message, she would have zero respect for me and there would be no chance of a comeback.

I also can hear some of you saying why not just block her when you are done? That's assertive, right? It is, but she's still left in the dark and the end result is the same, she's been ghosted and left wondering where it all went wrong.

I must caveat all of these points with saying I'd only tell women I don't want to see them where I had an established relationship with them. Usually after several months and where you've had sex. Of course, if you are travelling abroad and living a wonderous, debaucherous life with foreign stunners then no need to give them a dismissal over text. They know it's a one time, short term thing.

So, now that you're prepped to deliver the textual coup de grace, let's look at an example. For reference, the girl I'm texting is asking about my balls because I took a football to the nuts badly and had to go to hospital. Anyways, let's get to it!

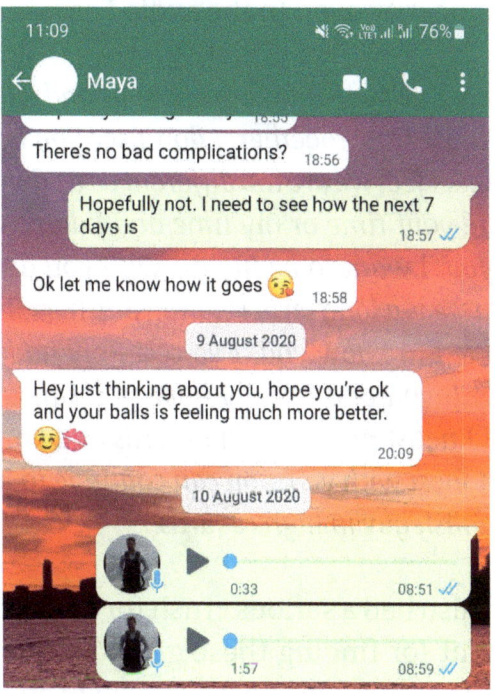

In this example, my breakup is communicated over the second audio message. I do an audio because we've been casually seeing each other for two months and I want to get more sincerity over. In the audio I say:

> *"Maya, I've been thinking about us and whilst I've enjoyed our time together, I don't see you being my girlfriend. I feel we are too different and I don't want to waste your time or my time and I don't want to ghost you. I want to be honest with you and don't think there is a long term relationship here. It's been nice to get to know you, I've certainly had a good time with you and I really hope you can continue to hold Englishmen in high regards and that by me being honest with you, you can continue to hold the next English guy in high regards."*

This girl also had a serious crush for Englishmen (I do have a talent for finding these girls 😊) and she regularly told me how much she fancied them and respected them. So, when I realised she wasn't for me at a time when I was looking for a long term relationship, I tell her straight. To be fair, she took it quite well and then a week later started texting me, asking me how I was etc. Since then, she hasn't blocked me and when she meets the next guy, she won't think all blokes are sneaky promisers of false hope, and if the next guy is English, well, he's in for a real treat 😉. Here's some texts you can use when you need to call it off.

> **Copy & Paste Zone**

> Hey (insert girls name), it's been great to get to know you over the last few months but I don't see us going any further. I wanted to be honest about it and not waste any more time.

> Hi, (insert girls name), I've had a think and I don't think we should continue to see each other. I don't want to set up false hopes and so wish you all the best with finding someone else.

16. Transitioning from Internet Dating Apps to Texting

"Swipe left, swipe right..."

WHILST I BELIEVE IN APPROACHING women face to face as the best way to meet them, I fully appreciate most men don't do this and prefer Internet Dating. Even though the method of meeting women is quite different here, you'll still need to text your matches if you want to go on dates and thus run into the same challenges as your approaching compatriots.

My main aim for messaging women when on Internet Dating apps is to get off the app as soon as possible and transition into WhatsApp. I'm adopting this methodology for two reasons. The first is, I'm screening for interest. Any reasonably attractive girl is getting hundreds or thousands of matches per week. Of these, she'll message a select few guys, but she won't be putting in much effort. If I match with her, I don't expect her to write much to me, but I do want to test her interest levels promptly. After a few messages, I'm giving her my mobile phone number and telling her to message me on WhatsApp. I've put the action on her and I move on. If she really is interested in me, she'll take the time to save my number in her contacts book and message me first.

This ties in nicely with the second reason to my methodology, saving time. I don't want to waste my time messaging a girl on an Internet Dating app if she is never going to go on a date with me. We referred to time wasters earlier in the book and these girls will happily message you for days and weeks, talking about just about anything except agreeing to going on a date with you. Furthermore, staying on the Internet Dating app is no effort for her and so she can happily while away your time in the message function without ever agreeing to a date with you.

This is my step-by-step process to transition from an Internet Dating app to WhatsApp:

1. We match
2. I send the opener and ask her something about her profile
3. She replies
4. I tell her to message me on WhatsApp and provide my number.

Here's an example from Tinder:

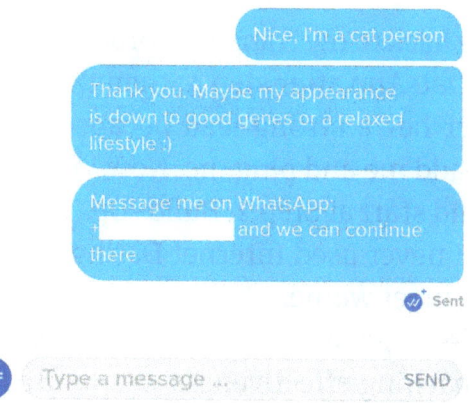

That's it. She'll either then add my number and ping me or she won't. She might moan a little after step 4 and say we should stay on the Internet Dating app to get to know each other better etc. However, I've moved on and am already messaging the next girl.

Now, some of you reading this might feel my methodology is too ruthless and that I should message more in the Internet Dating app to get to know the girl better, build more of a connection and increase the chance she'll transition into texting on WhatsApp. I do hear that point, and sometimes if I have the time, I'll run step 2 and 3 of my transition process once more, then go to step 4, however, my argument is Internet Dating is a visual marketplace. Interest is primarily derived from the photos provided by a person and to a much lesser extent, the written elements of the profile. Internet Dating was designed to be short and snappy. A quick tool to put two people in touch. I take it for what it is. If I match with a girl, she is saying she is interested. Even if it is vague and fleeting, there's something there. Let's test that attraction straight off the bat.

Coming back to my transition process, if she messages me on WhatsApp after step 4, then this is encouraging. I consider her a strong lead because she's taken the effort to add me and ping me. Now I follow the Texting Ladder and start at Step 2: Build-Up.

Whilst I never used Internet Dating apps as my main means to meet women, I did use them when abroad on holiday in large spaced out cities where I discovered my approaching effectiveness was limited from sparse streets. In this situation, I used Internet Dating apps in the background to complement face to face interactions. Similar to the street or bars, I'm screening for interest and prioritising my time.

I could write a whole book on Internet Dating and maybe one day I will, but for now, I'm swiping left 😊.

17. Thorpe's Texting Clinic – Troubleshooting

THIS CHAPTER IS DEDICATED TO solving the most frequently occurring problems men experience with texting. We hope you can flick to this chapter as and when you need to when you are not sure how to solve a particular problem.

17. 1. She won't text me back!

This is probably the most frustrating part of texting, especially if you really like a woman or worked really hard to get her number. We understand how hard this can be.

However, to put it simply, if she's not texting you back, she is not interested. As hard as it is to take, you need to face facts and move on. Repeatedly texting her and chasing will only push her further away. If you are referring to this sub-chapter because she hasn't texted you back and it's only been minutes, hours, or a day then relax! Most people lead busy lives and you need to be patient. Sometimes women will deliberately not text you back as a test. She is vacuuming you to see if you possess the virtue of patience. If you fill the void she has created and message again, you have just confirmed that you can't take the pressure and are not a high-value man. You have now stepped into her frame and your chances of going on a date with her are next to nil. The amount of times I have felt compelled to send a follow-up text to fill her silence, but have known better and adopted patience for her then to come through and text me back is infinite. This only validates my years of experience doing this.

My general rule is if I'm working my way up the Texting Ladder and she doesn't reply I leave it for a few days to allow her to come back to me. If she does not reply I'm back to Step 2 of the Texting Ladder and must begin climbing back up.

To try and make this second conversation stream more interesting I might kick it off with a photo ping or an audio message and recommence the conversation. You can see me explain this more on my YouTube channel, video titled 'How To Text A Girl Who Stopped Responding'.

If you feel you are in the last chance saloon or you are leaving her town shortly, you can try an honesty voice note or honesty text. This is a final pitch to get her out where you state the obvious in a relaxed manner; you thought she was nice and would like to go out with her. The theme you want to convey is that you want her but don't need her.

If she drops off again then she's simply not interested. There will be occasions where there is just cause for the girl not to text you back. She may have lost her phone, experienced a family emergency or just gone to ground for a few days working intensively on an assignment. These situations are rare, but they do happen. However, you won't know if this has happened, but she will judge you on your response. The best thing you can do is to send one follow-up message after a few days of silence, then leave it. Do not send more messages than this. When she does resurface, she will see you have sent one follow-up message but not gone mad in her absence and bombarded her phone with needy messages. If she's interested, she will message you back and probably apologise for her absence. Not chasing her in this window of silence will actually help you in the long run because you have just confirmed to her that you are a cool, relaxed guy who doesn't need her in your life to be happy and are satisfied with or without her messaging you back.

Women are complex creatures and their interest in you can vanish in an instant, either from something you did or said in your interaction or from other circumstances coming into play such as an ex coming back into her life or if she moves away to a new town etc. You can't control her interest levels or whether she replies to you. However, you can maximise the chances that she does reply to you and you do that by applying all the chapters of this book. Being a fun, interesting guy who is not outcome dependent on whether she texts you back is your best chance of her replying and you working your way up the Texting Ladder to securing that date.

17. 2. Her number doesn't work/I can't find her in my messaging app

This is a quick problem to solve. You've either entered the international prefix incorrectly or mistyped her number, in which case she's lost forever. You may also have forgotten her name and with a large contacts book it's like finding a needle in a haystack. Let's look at the most common problem first.

If, after taking a woman's phone number you didn't message her there and then, but preferred to wait till you got home and now can't find her on WhatsApp, Viber or Telegram, you probably have not added the international prefix correctly. To correct this, you need to know what country her phone number is associated with. If she's from the country you met her in, you can find out the correct international prefix from Google. For example, Brazil is +55. In this scenario, go to her entry in your contacts book and edit the number by removing the first zero and replacing with +55. Save it, then allow a few seconds or a minute before opening WhatsApp or Viber and searching for her name and voila! She should appear and you can message her.

If you've mistyped her number in your phone, then you've lost the contact forever and there's nothing we can do to help you. Take it as a lesson learnt and re-read Chapter 3. Collecting her number correctly is vital and you must not rush this moment.

If you are a bit of player and collect lots of phone numbers, then good on you! However, what if you can't find her number after a particularly busy street session or the following morning after a boozy night out. Worry not! Many app developers for both Apple and Android have produced apps that show you a list of all the phone numbers you have collected in time and date order. Win! Simply download one of these apps and have your memory jogged and commence texting.

To set yourself up correctly and make sure you never lose a number again re-read the Preamble Chapter.

17. 3. I didn't get her phone number, but I got her Facebook/Instagram/Email/LinkedIn. Do I still follow the chapters in this book?

In short, yes. However, at Team Thorpe if you tried to get her number and she gave you something else we consider that half of a number. And can you text half of a number? No you bloody can't. Realise that in this situation the girl has given you a polite blow-off and it's highly unlikely she will message you back.

When you are in the interaction in the street or the bar and you go for the number and she offers an alternative, recognise she is almost certainly playing games with you. If she is available and interested, you need to manage this test appropriately and ask for her phone number again. However, if she resists and offers Facebook or Instagram for example, the only tool left in your arsenal is to say you don't have Facebook or Instagram and to try for the phone number once more. If she still refuses or gives you an excuse, no matter what it is, she is not interested and you need to leave the interaction.

Only if she is your perfect type of woman and genuinely says that she only communicates through Facebook Messenger for example should you take this contact and close the interaction. Your chances of hearing from her are still minimal but you should always be closing.

17. 4. She rejected my date request, now what?

If she has rejected your date request, has she offered an alternative day or time? If yes, make a second date request matching her availability and book in the date. If no, as per the Texting Ladder in Chapter 2, you slide back down to Step 2 on the Ladder. Do not ask her out again and do not repeatedly text and chase her, trying to book her in. Recognise you are back to the beginning and take a day or two off from texting. Then, begin your climb back up the Texting Ladder. To make this second conversation a bit more interesting and dynamic, use photo pings or the occasional audio. Using these techniques might make the difference in getting her out on a date.

17. 5. How do I know if she has read my messages?

As per the Preamble Chapter, WhatsApp, Signal, Telegram and Viber offer the functionality of read receipts where you can see that she has read your message. However, these read receipts can be turned off leaving you none the wiser as to whether she has actually read your message. In this case, you will never know so the only thing you can do is stick to the Texting Ladder and practice the techniques in this book and progress towards getting her out on a date. WhatsApp, Signal, Telegram and Viber tell you the message has been delivered successfully so at least that's something. If you are using traditional SMS, you have no feedback as to whether she has received your message, let alone read it. In this case you have to trust you entered her number correctly into your phone. Re-read Chapter 3 to find some useful tools and techniques which you can practice to make sure you have captured her number correctly.

17. 6. I think I broke the conversation by being too needy or too smart. How do I fix this?

Vacuum. This is the only way to recover such a situation. Don't apologise, don't back pedal, and don't try to clarify yourself over more messages. Just vacuum and stay quiet. Depending on how much you feel you overstepped the mark dictates how long you should vacuum for. Generally, 3 days is a reasonable amount of time. If she fills your void and texts you, the conversation is back on and you can resume your climb back up the Texting Ladder. Don't restart the conversation with an apology or an explanation, just begin again as you normally would. If she hasn't replied during your vacuum period, consider leaving it a little longer. If after this extension she still hasn't come forward, send her an audio message or photo ping and try and restart the conversation. If she doesn't reply to this the conversation is dead and you will have learnt a valuable lesson. Re-read Chapter 6.

Recognise that we all make mistakes, even the pros. Texting too much, telling a joke that doesn't come off or giving too much of a push or pull are the most common pitfalls you can run into. You can't deliver a solid performance for every single texting conversation you have. As you practice the techniques in this book and become a better texter you will break less conversations and be more efficient in your communications. But for when you do mess it up, vacuum.

17. 7. I've got a date coming up and she hasn't entirely confirmed. Should I text her?

You are right to be concerned. Put simply, has she agreed to:

1. The day
2. The time
3. The specific location

If you don't have three yeses, then you have a problem. The most efficient way to book her in for a date is to send these three details in one message and she confirms. It's not necessarily wrong that you send and confirm these details over several messages, but each time you communicate the day, the time or the specific location she does need to reply to you and agree to each one. If you don't have three yes's and your date is fast approaching, she is probably having second thoughts and unfortunately does not possess the moral fibre to tell you straight. Assume the date is not happening. A few hours before the date you could send one of the following:

Copy & Paste Zone

> Hey, I'm on my way into the city.

> You ok for later?

> For later, I'll meet you by the big tree in the square.

The first example here is a fake logistical update. You're not actually heading to the date location, you just send this to jog her memory and indirectly remind her she has a date with you. This should compel her to confirm or cancel.

The second example is also fine on the morning of the date to see if she confirms.

The third example is providing some more specific date logistical information which is also indirectly checking to see if she is actually coming.

Sometimes I haven't had a girl give me the three yes's because she was so certain she was coming on the date she didn't feel the need to reply to one of my date logistic messages or simply forgot. Therefore, sending a quick clarification message is fine. However, if she doesn't reply to your confirmation text don't bother getting ready for the date and travelling to the location. Consider it a dead lead, archive her, and move on.

17. 8. Should I text her on the day of the date?

This depends on the certainty you have that she will turn up for the date and how your texting conversation has played out up until this point. If she has been texting back strongly and quickly, showing high levels of investment and she has agreed to the day, time and location as per the answer to question 17.7, then no, you do not need to send her a text to confirm she is coming.

However, if the texting conversation has been a tricky one to manage and where she may have previously refused your first date request, there is no harm in sending a quick confirmation text. See the Copy and Paste Zone to question 17.7.

If she doesn't reply to your confirmation message, then you need to decide how much you are going out of your way to meet her and what other plans you had. If the date location is not far away and doesn't cost you any money to get there then turn up and see if she does. If the date location is far away and costs a lot in public transport or a taxi, then I wouldn't recommend you go.

On a more positive note, you may find that she texts you on the day of the date to check you are still coming. This is a great sign and a simple reply of "*Yes, see you later*" will suffice.

If you have a date booked in, don't ruin it by sending an audio or a photo ping or by trying to recommence the texting conversation. You will only confuse her and undo all your hard work of getting the date booked in. Remember, the objective of texting is to get the girl out on a date. You have achieved your objective so don't text her!

17. 9. She won't agree to my date location and wants to go somewhere else. What should I do?

This is quite a common problem to encounter, particularly on the first date. Let's first look at her object of resistance. If you are proposing a date location that is good for you but far away for her and her investment level in you is average at best, expect resistance. She won't want to travel too far and spend money on public transport or a taxi while also thinking about how she will get home. Naturally, she will give you resistance and try and pull your date location to somewhere more central that is equidistant for both of you. There is also a subtle frame battle going on here. The simple solution here is that if you want to go on the date you will have to compromise and change your date location to somewhere more central and that is good for both of you. You haven't lost the frame, but on the date you will need to maintain assertiveness and build that connection up through rapport. Once you have done this you can move location whilst still on the date, moving back towards your town or house. This is covered on my website where you can learn everything you need to know about dating.

Logistics and location planning is king for dating so if you are lucky enough to live right in the centre of your town or city, or you are in an Airbnb or hotel when on holiday, you will largely eliminate this location resistance.

If you feel that she's a woman you are not seriously invested in and compromising on location puts you out of your way and you have other options with women then hold your line. You will probably lose her, but she may still come out after she has re-evaluated how much she wants to see you. To try and mitigate this problem in the future, you can probe her in the interaction or over text as to where she lives to garner this useful piece of information. This will help you when planning your dates.

17. 10. The conversation has hit a dead end. What should I do?

This is also another problem that you will frequently encounter, even for texting conversations that are going well. Similar to your conversations with friends or family face-to-face, the topic being discussed will naturally end. In real life what you do with your friends or family is change topic and move onto something else. Text messaging is no different. Don't keep ploughing a topic that has run its course. Take the initiative, draw a line under the conversation to date, change topic, and start a new conversation stream. Transitioning from one topic to another over text is easy. Simply start a new topic and if you want, use a photo ping or an audio message to help you with the transition.

Another technique you can adopt when the conversation has hit a dead end or heading towards one is to use the side-step. Texting conversations on controversial topics such as religion, politics, or your previous dating life with women are not topics you want to explore over text message. If you feel the conversation is sliding this way, break the thread by not answering her latest message and start a new conversation topic by sending an interesting photo ping about something completely different. This will serve as a distraction where you side-step the controversial topic and launch the conversation off into a new direction. Throughout all of this, keep one eye on where you are on the Texting Ladder. Side-stepping or naturally changing topic does not mean you start at the bottom of the Texting Ladder. You are still where you were, you're just pursuing a different conversation topic as you climb up the Texting Ladder.

17. 11. She's sending me one-word answers and making it difficult. What should I do?

You are right to show some concern here, especially as she is showing such low investment. However, I always come back to the Texting Ladder in such scenarios. When you text, is she replying? If the answer is yes, even if it's one word or very minimalistic answers you are progressing up the Texting Ladder. Put simply, if you are texting and she is replying you have a texting conversation on the go. Hang in there. You need to recognise that she might not be much of a texter or is just a bit lazy. Don't be deterred if she's not writing much back or asking you lots of questions. It may feel at times like the conversation will finish at any moment but you might be surprised: if you keep going you could work your way up to the top of the Texting Ladder and get her booked in for a date. Some of the hottest girls I have been out with were minimalistic texters. It's like they had read this book and realised that they only needed to do the minimum to advance the conversation onwards so did just that.

You can find out more about girls who reply with one word answers on my YouTube channel, video titled 'How To Text A Girl Who Replies With One Word'.

17. 12. I literally have no idea what to do next, help!
When you are starting out, this is the most common problem you will have so it's ok if you feel this way. However, the Texting Gods have provided you with this book so at least you have something! If you are lost as to what to do next, simply refer to the Texting Ladder. It's a fail-safe, universal structure to guide you. See which step you think you are on and go forward from that point. Don't get drawn away into her games or conversation topics and stick closely to the Texting Ladder structure. Re-read the chapters we have provided for you. Could you send a photo ping or is time to breathe some life into the conversation with an audio message? Has the conversation run its

course and you need to change topic? If the conversation has gone a bit flat and you feel you are coming across a bit too nice, it's time to create a reaction with some push-pull. Maybe you've come across too strongly, in this case it's time to vacuum. Texting is supposed to be simple so try and adopt that mindset. You are not trying to prove that you are a modern-day Shakespeare and woo her over text message. Texting's sole objective is to get her out on a date, so do the minimum to advance the conversation onto the next step up the Texting Ladder.

17. 13. She's texting loads and super interested, how do I not mess it up?

In this scenario it can be easy to get excited and overinvest in the texting conversation, spoiling the interaction. What you need to do is keep calm and stick to the Texting Ladder. Don't try and cheat the system by asking her out straight away. You will almost certainly fall from whichever step you are on and may not be able to recover the conversation. Managing a super keen woman is covered in Chapter 2.7 – mirroring, so re-read this. Be aware that the positivity and investment can be so high you may find you are both typing at the same time. That is like two people walking through a door at the same time which never works! If you see this happening, stop texting and allow her to type and send her messages. Leave it a few minutes. You may find she pauses, then starts typing again and sends you even more messages. You must give a woman the time and space to express herself. Don't interrupt her. Then, when you feel she has said what she wants, reply. Leaving a gap of just a few minutes is invaluable and means you can digest all that she is writing whilst maintaining your grip on the frame. Capitalise on this positive energy and stick to climbing up the Texting Ladder. You could get her booked in for a date in a very short space of time.

17. 14. I'm on holiday for a few days and don't feel I have the time to follow the Texting Ladder structure. Is there a way I can fast track the process and get women out on dates so I don't run out of time?

Yes. In such scenarios you need to change your approach to texting. If you were to rigorously follow the Texting Ladder, as you would do in your hometown, it may take several days for you to work your way up to the date request and head out on a date. With time against you, after you have sent your Step 1: Opener and she has replied, send the Step 3: Date Feeler and move the conversation on.

You could also send an audio message like the ones we described in Chapter 8. You would simply say something along the lines that you are leaving soon, but you thought she seemed nice and that you want to go for a drink with her. Keep the audio message short and brief. You wouldn't necessarily need to ask her out through a question over the audio message. Simply stating that you like her, you want to go for a drink, and offering some availability is a good way to go about it. If she's keen, she'll come back to you. Alternatively, you could put the content of this type of audio message into a text, laying your cards out on the table as you approach the end of your holiday. You might want to do this if her English is not very good or non-existent.

The other scenario where you can jump up the Texting Ladder is when you are in a big party environment or festival, such as Rio Carnival. These types of events last for days where normal social etiquette is sidelined in favour of living for the moment and being free spirited. If you find yourself in a Carnival or a big party event and you have collected some phone numbers, you can send your Step 1: Opener texts and then, once the women reply, go straight for the Step 4: Date Request. By reflecting the loose and fast social scene, you won't harm your chances going straight for the date request. At such big parties and festivals no one is really operating to a tight, organised schedule and equally the women you meet can easily vanish for the rest of your holiday as they get sucked into the fun party vibes. They will also be busy enjoying themselves and not spending hours on their phones. So, sending the opener then going for the date request is the most effective way to text in such environments. Your best chances of going on dates is often the same day you met or that evening, so moving quickly and jumping up the Texting Ladder is fine on these occasions.

Only if your holiday is coming to an end or you are engrossed in a big South American Carnival can you exclude yourself from the Texting Ladder structure.

17. 15. She's not texting back and I think the lead is dead. Is there anything more I can do to try and revive the conversation?

Yes. This technique has also been called "Raising the Dead", though our explanation will be far less sinister. If your texting conversation has stopped and the lead has gone cold, we recommend sending a photo ping or audio message to try and revive the conversation in the first instance. If this doesn't work, then you could delete a message you have just sent to spark her interest. To explain the specifics, I will use WhatsApp as the example. Go into the chat you want to revive and make sure the girl is not online. Then, type a quick message, such as "*abc*" and send it. Once the message has been delivered, immediately select the message by holding your finger down on it and select the option "delete for everyone." This will delete your message and leave a notification on the chat saying you deleted this message. When she is next online, she will see your chat at the top of her list of chats and see that you deleted your message. If she has any ounce of interest in you, she will be baited by your hidden message and want to find out what it is you have sent. Enticing her in this way may encourage her to send you a message, asking what it is you meant to say. You have just restarted the conversation. Don't answer her question and return back to the Texting Ladder, recommencing the conversation towards a date request. The chances of this happening successfully are slim, but it can work and it's a very quick and easy way to test for those remaining levels of interest.

   I also cover this technique on my YouTube Channel, video titled 'How To Text A Girl Who Ghosted You – WhatsApp Deletion Technique'

18. Putting It All Together - In Closing

"Do, or do not, there is no try."

IN THIS BOOK I HAVE shown you everything you need to know to be successful at texting women. No matter where you are on your journey, I hope this book has helped you and will continue to help you in being a practical source of information and a fountain of knowledge for all your texting needs. Through these chapters I have imparted my 9 years of experience texting over a thousand women. Hopefully you can see that there's a lot more to texting than just sending a quick, *"hi, how are you?"*

Love it or hate it, texting rightfully takes its place as a cornerstone of your approach in pursuing women. You may well be good at approaching or swiping and collecting numbers, but if you cannot text as a high-value man should, you won't be dating these women. Texting is not to be underestimated and, although it appears insignificant to many, one false move from you and your conversation will be over in a heartbeat with the woman of your dreams. Use this book to keep yourself in the game, progress up the Texting Ladder and head out on those dates.

I've shared the Texting Ladder with you; a fail-safe, universal structure that should be your go to reference point at all times when texting women. It looks simple, and that's because it is. Follow the sequence of steps I have described and you won't go wrong. In support of this, I have also shared with you all the key tools and techniques every man should know to complement the Texting Ladder. From the basics, such as asking less questions, to the more advanced techniques of push-pull, audio messaging and phone calls, there is a whole skillset to learn, practice, and build. If you can add these skills to your texting repertoire you will be way ahead of other men, demonstrating your value to women as someone they want to meet. Of course, you will encounter problems and find your limits along your texting journey. For this, the troubleshooting chapter will hopefully help you solve the most commonly occurring problems. And always remember that unseen principle: frame. Drive your conversations forward from a strong, assertive frame where you want her, but you don't need her. You are a busy man about town who has plenty of other interesting pursuits to occupy him. Women and texting are just one part of that frame.

Texting should be simple and, as I said in the beginning, is a means to get a woman out on a date. Nothing more. Follow the techniques described in this book and you will start going out on dates. You don't need to tell her your life story and you don't need to try and impress her. You just need to do the bare minimum to advance the conversation. Women will expect you to know what you are doing and they are not going to educate you on any of this. It's down to you to improve yourself and your abilities.

Your challenge now is to bring all of these tools and techniques together. If you can do this you will come across as direct, assertive, interesting, mischievous and confident. And all the while operated from a strong, masculine, unbreakable frame. The real art with texting is to know what to do, when to do it and why in any given scenario. A man who knows all of this can calibrate himself to any text messaging conversation and confidently take the correct course of action. Knowing where he is at all times on the Texting Ladder and knowing what texting technique to employ at a particular moment is key. Thus, he is a calibration master. This should be your goal for texting. Get to this level and texting women will become seamless. This book goes a long way in helping you to become your very own calibration master. But the truth to anything worth earning in life is to apply dedication, resilience, and most importantly of all, hard work.

From all of us at Team Thorpe, happy texting!

Review This Book

★★★★★

DID YOU LIKE THIS BOOK? If yes, please write a short review on Google here:

Your feedback is hugely appreciated and helps other guys decide if this book is for them. If you didn't enjoy the book, please email me at: davidthorpe@davidthorpe-dating.com and tell me why. All feedback is appreciated.

YouTube & Social Media

YouTube Channel

Follow me as I teach you how to meet, date and attract your dream girlfriend. Focusing on the four cornerstones of a man's dating life, I teach men how to approach, how to text, how to date and how to transition into that long term relationship you always wanted. I provide entertaining and educational content on all things dating and post new content every week. Check out my channel and don't forget to subscribe!

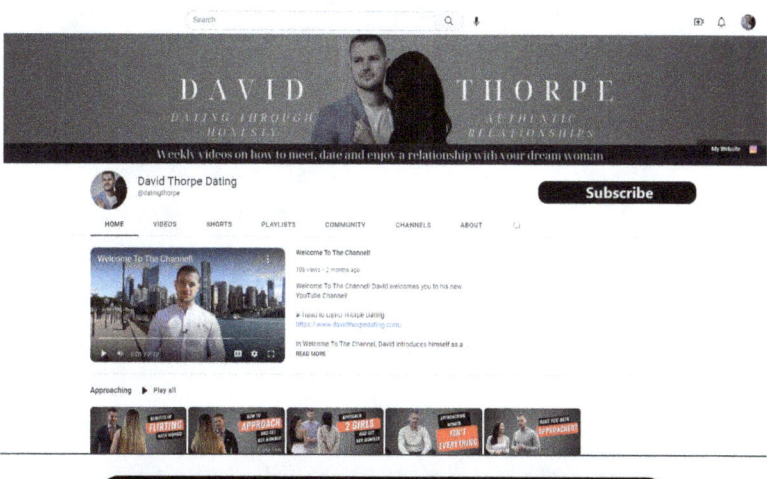

Instagram: instagram.com/datingthorpe/

Tik Tok: tiktok.com/@davidthorpedating

Facebook: facebook.com/datingthorpe

More Dating Resources

APPROACHING

You see your dream woman but can't approach?

Can't say hi?

You would love to be able to approach your perfect girl. You see her and imagine that you can confidently walk over, pay her a compliment, strike up a fun conversation and ask her out and do all this, without coming off weird or creepy.

However, the reality is you just stand there, freeze and do nothing. She walks on by and you've wasted yet another opportunity.

If this is you and you're really determined to fix this area of your dating life then you can and I'd love to be able to help you.

Being able to approach far outstrips internet dating and puts you head and shoulders above the rest of men in the eyes of women.

The experience of learning how to approach is honestly, life changing. Don't waste any more time!

So, if you want to learn how to approach, how to do so respectfully, and be comfortable with women around you, then head over to my website where you can learn everything you need to know about approaching.

www.davidthorpedating.com

DATING

Getting dates isn't a problem for you but you're running into problems. From being stood up, to not knowing what to do on the date, you can't take her home or can't secure that second date; you have issues with dating. Head over to my website where you can learn everything you need to know about dating.

www.davidthorpedating.com

About the Author

NINE YEARS AGO, DAVID'S DATING life was at breaking point. Rapidly approaching his 26th birthday he was alone and realised that if he didn't do something he would be condemned to a solitary life. This, to him, seemed unfair because he was forging a career that he loved, had good friends, a supportive family and an excellent lifestyle in London. On the surface everything seemed fine but, it wasn't.

When it came to women and dating, David was useless, shy, crippled with a lack of confidence and was not happy. Back then, he'd get around 2 phone numbers a year and go on one date that would go nowhere. Women were not a part of David's life.

Change needed to come and David was determined to find it.

In 2013 David went on a dating bootcamp where he learned to approach.

He spent 2 full days approaching women in London, applying the system his coaches had developed. He collected 8 phone numbers that weekend and now had options with women. All David needed was to be shown the way and given a little push.

There was just 10 weeks to go until Christmas and David was determined to consolidate his newfound skillset and never return to his old dating ways. He went out every Saturday and Sunday, approaching morning, noon and night. Phone numbers started to turn into texting conversations, which turned into dates and just before Christmas, David started to bring women home. He had changed, and there was no going back.

The following years David met a lot of women and had success, but something wasn't right.

He was feeling hollow and empty, was having scripted conversations and didn't feel genuine. So, being honest with himself he had his first realisation. The only real change David had made to his dating life was being able to approach and believing that he could change this area of his life. The hollow emptiness and lack of genuineness he was feeling was coming from saying lines, following rigid structures and not being himself. So, David dropped the lines and structures and brought more of his personality back into his interactions, instantly feeling freer and more authentic. His results with women skyrocketed. Saying lines was not the solution, David himself was.

What followed in David's late twenties and early thirties was fantastic, happy times.

He travelled the world with belief in himself and led a single life most men could never dream of. From Eastern Europe, the Middle East to Asia and South America David met some of the world's hottest, most personable women and had a lot of fun. He wouldn't have spent the time any other way. With his newfound confidence David enjoyed success in other areas of his life, particularly in his career which went from strength to strength and he bought his first house in London.

Several years ago, David met his truly amazing wife from a cold approach on the streets of Sydney, Australia. After a while they started a relationship and since then have gone from strength to strength. David didn't know it was possible to be this happy and for him, she is exactly the kind of woman he wants to be in a relationship with.

David's dream life with women wasn't achieved by some secret system. It came from being honest with himself and being honest with women. Thus, his motto, "Dating through honesty" was born. This, David believes, is the key to a successful dating life and a happy long-term relationship.

Contact Me

For any questions, troubleshooting or feedback on the book, reach out to David Thorpe at

davidthorpe@davidthorpedating.com

www.ingramcontent.com/pod-product-compliance
Lightning Source LLC
Chambersburg PA
CBHW071233170426
43191CB00032B/1363